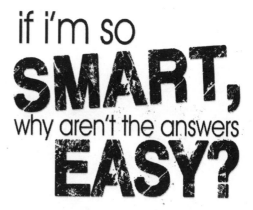

if i'm so
# SMART,
why aren't the answers
# EASY?

if i'm so
# SMART,
why aren't the answers
# EASY?

Advice From Teens on Growing Up Gifted

**Robert A. Schultz, Ph.D., &**
**James R. Delisle, Ph.D.**

PRUFROCK PRESS INC.
WACO, TEXAS

# Dedication

Bob dedicates this book to Brendon and Caytlin. I may know giftedness from "catching" it and studying it, but you really don't know giftedness until you have to *live* with it! And to Cindy, what can I say? There is a special place in heaven waiting for you. You live with it *times three*!

Jim dedicates this book, his 17th, to the same people to whom he dedicated his first book, in 1983: "Deb and Matt, for their continuous love and sharing." Same words . . . identical sentiment.

Library of Congress Cataloging-in-Publication Data

Schultz, Robert A., 1962-
If I'm so smart, why aren't the answers easy? / by Robert A. Schultz and James R. Delisle.
   p. cm.
ISBN 978-1-59363-960-0 (pbk.)
1. Gifted teenagers. 2. Gifted persons. I. Delisle, James R., 1953- II. Title.
BF724.3.G53S377 2013
155.5'1398--dc23

                              2012022967

Edited by Lacy Compton

Production design by Raquel Trevino

ISBN-13: 978-1-59363-960-0

At the time of this book's publication, all facts and figures cited are the most current available. All telephone numbers, addresses, and website URLs are accurate and active. All publications, organizations, websites, and other resources exist as described in the book, and all have been verified. The authors and Prufrock Press Inc. make no warranty or guarantee concerning the information and materials given out by organizations or content found at websites, and we are not responsible for any changes that occur after this book's publication. If you find an error, please contact Prufrock Press Inc.

Prufrock Press Inc.
P.O. Box 8813
Waco, TX 76714-8813
Phone: (800) 998-2208
Fax: (800) 240-0333
http://www.prufrock.com

# TABLE OF CONTENTS

# ACKNOWLEDGMENTS
## Merci Beaucoup!

We want to thank the many thousands of gifted individuals the world over who contributed to our understanding about giftedness by responding to our questionnaires at http://www.giftedkidspeak.com, sending us their stories about growing up gifted, and talking to us while we are teaching, presenting at conferences, or sometimes, just hanging out for fun.

The contributors of the longer stories and insights in this book hold a special place in our hearts and minds. You inspire us to continue our work with your spot-on stories and experiences. Thank you for taking the time to share. You may not know it yet, but you've touched the future through these pages.

And, to our families, the resilience to carry on with the grand task of birthing a book is nothing short of miraculous. Without your patience, kindness, and willingness to endure periods of hysteria, joy, and sometimes generalized crankiness, this project would never have come to fruition.

# INTRODUCTION

WE live in a world obsessed with speed—the quickest network, the broadest coverage, cloud computing, and even food that can't seem to be served or eaten fast enough. While inhaling said food, you can retrieve answers to any question or gain entry to the world's largest repository of information in a virtual instant via the Internet and handheld devices.

Yet, when it comes to understanding—or even defining—giftedness, we seem to be in no rush to get there.

For more than a century, giftedness (and its "close cousin," talent development) has been studied. Literally millions of words have been written *describing* this construct. Yet, the majority of people who have taken the time to study high intelligence and ability have done so from afar—a research lab, a university classroom, or a counselor's office. Although there is nothing wrong with learning about the idea of giftedness from these places, the people who best know both the high points and the hurdles of giftedness are the teens who wear the "gifted" label. No doubt, a teen like you.

In the pages that follow, you will have the opportunity to "meet" giftedness through the voices and experiences of teens and young adults bearing that label. They share their stories, insights, anxieties, and joys, and they give some advice about growing up gifted from their own personal perspectives.

In addition to the hundreds of student comments encased within these pages, you'll also find Your Turn boxes throughout the book. We created these reflective activities with the hope that they would enable and encourage you to see giftedness through your own experiences with this label. We hope that in completing some of these exercises, you will find out even more about your giftedness and how it impacts (or can impact) your life.

# HOW THIS BOOK
# CAME TO BE

As university professors, researchers, and teachers, we spend a lot of time reading the literature associated with giftedness. One limitation we constantly find is that people talk about giftedness and make statements or give advice based on what *they* think giftedness means. But very little of this advice comes directly from gifted students.

So, beginning in 2003, we asked gifted individuals around the world to share their beliefs, experiences, and concerns by responding to questionnaires on our website (http://www.giftedkidspeak.com). The process continues to this day, with tens of thousands of individuals having shared their thoughts thus far.

In *If I'm So Smart, Why Aren't the Answers Easy?*, we focus on sharing stories *from* gifted teens, *for* gifted teens. What you'll find between this book's covers are representative answers, unique stories, and some interesting insights from more than 5,000 teens and young adults who took the time to answer our questionnaires.

You'll also find some more elaborate stories from gifted teens and young adults about the paths they have taken—or not taken—in coming to terms with their own high intelligence and abilities. We have learned time and time again that gifted individuals, as unique as each one is, share many thoughts and beliefs when it comes to school, friends, expectations, and life in general. Our hope is that in reading these stories, you will recognize some elements from them in you. We *know* these teens . . . and we think you should, too.

Even in a world as fast-paced as ours, slowing down to consider the person you are, and the one you hope to become, seems to us a worthwhile task. We hope you agree.

# chapter 1

# WHAT IS GIFTEDNESS?

**THE** definition of giftedness is one of the most hotly debated topics by anyone having any interest in ability. In fact, within the field of gifted education, experts have yet to agree upon a common set of gifted behaviors and tendencies—let alone clearly state a distinction between being gifted and/or talented.

Is giftedness real? What does the term mean?

We believe giftedness is a state of being, and it is real. We also know that being labeled affects your life (more than just at school!). Is it something you will outgrow? Can you be cured?

We needed help in setting the record straight. So we asked gifted individuals around the world to help us answer these questions. And here's a sampling of what was said.

What do you think being gifted means? What is your reaction to the term "gifted"?

Being gifted means an ability to learn things faster. My reaction to the term is "I'm not gifted." I just work hard. I think calling exceptionally smart people "gifted" takes credit away from their hard work and effort and says, "they were just born that way."

—Girl, 13, Oklahoma

**Gifted is like the plague. You get identified and everyone around you changes the way you are treated. Isn't there another way to say I'm bright and quick instead of the invisible tattoo?**

**—Boy, 13, West Virginia**

Giftedness is having exceptional abilities and being motivated enough to use those abilities to create wonderful things.

—Girl, 13, Iowa

**Being gifted is: Grandiose, Gorgeous, Gigantic, Galactic. Of course I don't share this lexicological alliteration often—I need to fit in!**

**—Boy, 14, Rhode Island**

My reaction toward the term "gifted"? I basically think of nerds, which means I think I am a nerd, but also, at the same time, I don't feel like one.

—Girl, 14, Texas

**Personally, I don't think that being picked out as gifted is anything special. I think being gifted is just a fable that teachers use to give us harder work.**

**—Boy, 14, Nebraska**

Being gifted is a state of mind. It is liking adult (not rude, but more mature) humor, debating issues, being interested in the world, and wanting to make a difference. It's wanting to be perfect.

—Girl, 14, England

**What gifted means to me is that my brain works so much faster than most people around me that it is hard to maintain interest in conversations. (Why is it so hard to state this fact without sounding like I'm bragging or lying?)**

**—Boy, 14, North Carolina**

Being gifted means getting to miss class and do fun stuff in elementary school and being bored in class in later years. It means nothing other than adults need a euphemism for "smart" because they can't say I'm "smart" and put me in the "smart classes" that my parents were in in the 1960s and 1970s.

—Girl, 15, Wisconsin

**Being gifted means being recognized for my inquisitiveness and drive to know things.**
**It means I live life to the fullest, and this causes envy in others.**
**—Girl, 15, South Dakota**

My reaction to the word gifted is always the same: "Are you talking to *me?*"
—Boy, 16, Ohio

# YOUR TURN

Many gifted people have a negative view about the term "gifted." Some think it is elitist, others find it vague, and a few see it as just (as one student responded) "a fable that teachers use to give us harder work." How do you see it? If you don't like the term, what do you suggest as a replacement? If you do like the term gifted, tell us why.

**Gifted can't really be defined, in my opinion. It means something slightly different to everyone, with gifted people being even more diverse in their definitions than anyone else.**

**—Boy, 16, Iowa**

Gifted means you can forget to study and still do well on "the big test."

—Girl, 16, Texas

**Being gifted is a joy when I'm around people who understand that labels are only cheap ways to compare people. It is horrible when the comparisons pit divergent groups against one another.**

**—Boy, 16, Colorado**

It means I'm smart. It also means I wear my heart on my sleeve. Others see the former, but totally miss the latter. I don't just "get over it." It's who I am.

—Girl, 16, Nebraska

**I do not like the term "gifted." I believe it puts young people on a platform that is not always earned.**

**—Boy, 17, Tennessee**

It is difficult to define giftedness because there are so many degrees of difference.

—Girl, 17, Nevada

**Being gifted, I can form connections in ways that your average student can't. When I learn something in history class that relates to something in English class, I have a much better chance of putting two and two together.**

**—Boy, 18, Virginia**

I always hated the term "gifted." I was always more or less set apart from the other kids in school, and being labeled gifted just made it worse. It gave them one more thing to tease me about.

—Girl, 19, North Carolina

What would "gifted" be? Faster, quicker, deeper? Motivated, self-challenged, driven? This sounds like a professional athlete—and we know they can't be gifted. After all—people look up to them, but ridicule or ignore us.

—Girl, 19, Arizona

## How did you find out that you are gifted?

My parents stumbled across a friend of a friend who knows a gifted kid when he saw one. We met. We talked. He said I was definitely a candidate. Next thing you know, I take a couple tests and here I am, a newly gifted kid. Funny, I don't feel any different!

—Boy, 12, Vermont

**I always knew. I was always different from the other kids.**

—Girl, 13, New Jersey

What kind of question is this? It's not like I'm a mutation or something. It's not like "one day I looked at a test, and *it was really easy!*" Gifted is just something you are.

—Boy, 13, Massachusetts

**I never "found out." People just told me I was smart. They bussed me far away to be with other "smart kids." They kept telling us we were gifted, different, set apart. So I learned to be that way.**

—Girl, 14, Minnesota

I took a Midwest Talent Search Test on a whim since a friend needed the comfort of company. I guess you could say I earned my identification in the service of another.

—Boy, 14, Illinois

**Research. I simply saw what I was doing, what others were doing, did a bit of digging around, generated a lot of questions, and came to the conclusion that I probably qualified as gifted. I mean they were reading** *Clifford*; **I was reading** *Hamlet*.

—**Girl, 14, Australia**

When I met other family members, their first comment would be, "So, this is the genius?"

—Boy, 15, Utah

**In school, I had a system: pay attention on Monday, then daydream and doodle until Friday, when I would pass whatever tests they gave me, because it was reviewed the whole week. I hated it. So my mother had me tested, they figured I was gifted, and I went to a different school.**

—**Girl, 15, Connecticut**

I went to a summer camp for gifted kids (even though I was not) to learn about forensics. It was great fun, and I fit right in. In the fall, I was invited into our school's GT program. I guess some of the giftedness must have rubbed off on me.

—Boy, 15, Ohio

## YOUR TURN

Some say it was a test. Others seemed to know they were different from a young age. Finding out you are gifted can be a relief or cause stress in your life. We'd like you to get in the mix with your thoughts. Develop a three-step plan you would use to identify the gifted. Include answers you would give to kids (and parents) who were just identified if they asked, "So what does this all mean? What do I/we do next?"

A psychologist tested me and found that I had a blisteringly high IQ—and wasn't suffering from Oppositional Defiant Disorder. School was just too damn slow! (Sorry!)

—Girl, 15, California

I didn't really understand what giftedness was until seventh grade, at which point my giftedness combined with my "cavalier attitude" to create the biggest clash I've ever had with . . . well, anything.

—Boy, 16, Iowa

I pretty much knew when I went to school. I like to know rules of games before you play, not make them up as you go. I also was reading when everyone else was learning letters. It was so boring.

—Girl, 16, Kansas

One day, the gifted fairy came to my bedside and whispered in my ear the magic words to become gifted. The next day when I woke up, I had an intense headache, which would later be identified as my brain growing to an enormous size. (In other words, I was noticed in seventh grade for my creativity.)

—Boy, 16, Tennessee

I was always a loner. I loved to read and write, while a lot of my friends wanted to talk and text. Once I joined a writer's group in my city, everything fell into place. I knew then I wasn't weird. I've been flying high ever since.

—Girl, 16, New Jersey

When I was released into "regular" public school from my special ed classes in my inner-city neighborhood school, I noticed that many of the kids considered me "smart" and a "nerd," despite my Goth/slacker image.

—Girl, 17, New York

When I was in elementary school, I was in a Spanish immersion program. One of the classes taught in Spanish was math. When it became clear that not only did I have a better grasp on math than my teacher, but that I spoke better Spanish than she did, despite it being her first language and my second, there wasn't much doubt in anyone's mind.

—Boy, 17, Virginia

# THE PROS AND CONS OF GIFTEDNESS

Once upon a time, the aristocracy looked after the interests of the general population. These learned individuals—since they had the leisure time and finances for an education—were expected to rule benevolently and provide protection. In return, the local population paid tribute—mostly in the form of crops or labor for the aristocrats. It was a community affair, where everyone depended upon one another.

Fast forward 700 years . . .

Communities pay tribute to their local sports teams and in return receive entertainment as an escape from the drudgeries of their common lives. Everyone is in competition and society relies on currency and credit as a means of trade and wealth. Finances measure power and prestige, and almost everyone believes competition is the way to improve your lot in life.

In the past, the gifted were revered for their abilities to contribute to the betterment of the local community. In the present, the gifted are reviled for their abilities to outshine community members. That is, unless you are an athlete, as noted above.

Where are we headed with this history lesson? We believe gifted individuals struggle with their abilities in a society that doesn't necessarily feel compelled to care. Most of this struggle leads to negative outlooks on life and other people.

We want to bring this issue into the open and change this mindset. Our goal is to provide some hope and a positive look at life. Let's start with what gifted teens have to say.

## What are the best and worst parts about being gifted?

Best? I get to hold intelligent conversations with intelligent people. Also, I have enough intelligence to control my life and where I want to go with it. Worst? Discrimination. My abilities are held against me.

—Girl, 13, Australia

**The best part is being able to manipulate people to get what I want. The worst part is the guilt associated with being able to manipulate people to get what I want.**

**—Girl, 14, Ontario, Canada**

The best thing is how much you can learn. The worst thing is that you aren't learning it.

—Boy, 14, Massachusetts

**The best part is the recognition. The worst is the brand on my forehead. What? You can't see it? It seems everyone else can. I feel like a leper sometimes with so few people I can turn to. That necessary solitude must be the worst thing.**

**—Girl, 14, Texas**

The worst is the loneliness associated with the complexity of my mind. I haven't found any best [thing] yet . . . but I hope to one day.

—Boy, 14, North Dakota

**The best part is that you know you have an above-average ability to make positive changes in society by using your talents. The worst thing is not really having a choice in the matter and not knowing whether you can take credit for something that seems mainly enabled by accident of birth.**

**—Girl, 14, Massachusetts**

The best thing is I enjoy certain things meant for older and more educated people. The worst is, people treat me like I'm better and different.

—Boy, 15, California

**The best is boisterous recognition of subtle humor in my [GT] classes. There's nothing worse than cracking up at a pun while everyone stares at you coldly.**

**—Girl, 15, Washington**

Usually, my brain is my favorite playmate, but occasionally it turns traitor on me just when I need it the most. I hate that. I really can't address this question any better than this, because since I've always been gifted, I have no basis for comparison. Do I ask other people what it's like to be average?

—Boy, 15, North Carolina

**The best thing is all the doors it opens and all the recognition you get. The worst is also all the possibilities, because I have trouble choosing what I want to do—and people expect me to know.**

**—Girl, 15, Iowa**

The worst is knowing I can do anything I put my mind to but not knowing where or how to start. It is stressful and personally humiliating.

—Boy, 15, New Hampshire

The best thing about being gifted is knowing that I am not mentally deranged or otherwise atypical. I worried about why I was so different from other kids—obsessed about it really. Once I was identified and began meeting other highly gifted individuals, I felt a sense of calm. There were other people like me. It was wonderful to know.

—Girl, 15, Belgium

The best thing about being called gifted? It looks good on college applications, I guess.

—Boy, 16, Tennessee

The absolute best is being accepted into adult conversations on politics, ethics, and world events. I used to be always told to go play with the other kids, but once I was gifted, my interest was accepted.

—Girl, 16, Maryland

Best: The teachers love us because we're the "good" kids. Worst: People judge you before they even know you.

—Girl, 16, Oklahoma

Best: A lot of things come easily to me. Worst: The high expectations never go away.

—Boy, 16, Wisconsin

Best: Being with intellectual peers who don't fret your endless questions and esoteric interests. Worst: Living in a society whose focus is on making sure all the blades of grass measure up to a level height and focuses on cutting off any [that are] higher than average.

—Girl, 16, Hawaii

The loneliness is the worst. I'm from a very small school in a rural area and there aren't many other gifted kids around. I struggle with issues like religion, morality, philosophy, and politics, and there simply isn't anyone I can talk to about them. It leads me

**to feel I am very, very, very alone in this world. The best thing is the level of complexity I can comprehend. I love hard concepts that make me reorganize my ways of thinking. Sometimes, when the ideas are coming fast and heavy, it feels like my brain is dancing.**

**—Boy, 17, Kansas**

The worst was the relative ease I had in high school. I never learned to study and this nearly unwound me at college. Thank you very much for Freshman Forgiveness!

—Girl, 18, Ohio

When most people hear the term "giftedness," the first thing that comes to mind has something to do with mental acuity—the ability to understand ideas more quickly or at a deeper level than others your age. Although this interpretation is adequate, it is not necessarily sufficient. Why not? Because it's impossible to section off one part of your existence—in this case, your intellect—from other parts of yourself.

In this first-person essay, you'll be introduced to someone who is very good at thinking on his feet—and is equally adept at "thinking on his skates." Brendon Schultz shares some of the frustrations he feels when playing ice hockey with teammates whose mental abilities actually hinder their physical ones. Brendon raises some important questions that relate to both the benefits and drawbacks of team sports for someone like him, who is equally skilled with his mind and his body. As you read Brendon's essay, think of any nonacademic situations (such as sports, musical performances, or dance) in which you have found some frustrations similar to Brendon's. How have you coped with these? Who have you gone to for guidance or to express your desire for competition that actually challenges your own abilities?

# Brendon Schultz
## Feeling "Stuck" in Sports

A big part of who I am—my giftedness—is that I am a very quick thinker and very intense. This has an impact on my academics, but really shows up in sports. My giftedness helps me do drills and run plays faster, because I understand what to do the first or second time we are shown something by the coaches. I process information faster so I see things a lot quicker than other kids—even older players. (I know this because I play "up" with guys older than me.)

For instance, in lacrosse I make quick passes and find open space faster than other players. I look before I have the ball and read/recognize the defense. This lets me make better plays when I do get the ball. As an Attack, this is key to getting goals or feeding the Middies coming down through the slot to the net.

In hockey, I see the ice really well, but this is also sometimes frustrating. The game is about taking advantage of the other team's mistakes. I can read this quickly, but for most kids I've played with, the game seems to move too fast and they can't mentally keep up or read ahead. It's like I am moving smooth while other kids are playing in glue.

It is really irritating when players on my team make the same mistakes over and over. They never seem to learn from the mistakes, which means we are caught as a team many times by the other team pressuring the puck. Or, we have to go through drills during practice many, many times before being able to work on refining things.

My frustration at having to continually repeat drills or endure mistakes in games makes me not want to play sometimes. They are team sports, so I know I can't just do everything myself—even though I sometimes try because I am intense! This makes things worse because when I work without support, things can get ugly on the field or ice. I know it is only a game, but sometimes my intensity really ratchets up, and performance becomes very personal to me.

I can process what is going on fast—sometimes (this might sound conceited) faster than even coaches see it. This causes some trouble when I get excited on the bench while trying to share what is happening or is going to happen.

In a perfect world, I could match up lines and make our team better during the game based on knowledge of the opponent and tendencies they show during play. In a perfect world, our players and coaches would hear the information I am sharing and make adjustments because they would know I have a great feel for the game and the intensity to perform.

What keeps me going in sports is comments I hear from coaches. For instance, my ice skating coach, who played hockey professionally, says that I see the game better than a lot of the guys he played with in the pros, and, that I have a good chance to play at a high level. It boosts my confidence when I hear this.

But it can also be frustrating. Sometimes I feel stuck, like I'm not growing or getting better because I want to react to what is going on during shifts but can't—our team can't. The other players just don't see the ice or field like I do or lack the intensity to make adjustments to win.

I want to play hockey at the highest level I can reach. I want to win a state championship. I'd like to play in college and beyond—but that is a long way off and a lot of work ahead. I know I can make it if I can keep from getting too frustrated.

I am curious to know if there are other gifted teens who have the same sorts of frustrations. I don't know many gifted kids at all who play sports at a highly competitive level. So, my experience might be way off from what most teens feel. I don't know how to think about this. In a lot of ways it makes me sad. If I am the only one who has this ability to see things quickly and react quickly, what chance am I ever going to have to use this to the highest capacity if everyone else on my teams lag behind? I don't know the answer, but I do worry about it.

*Brendon Schultz is a 14-year-old sophomore attending a private college prep school where he is content accelerated 4 years in mathematics and also takes junior-level Honors courses. He plays competitive travel hockey and lacrosse for his high school.*

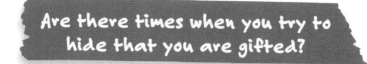
No way. I never try to hide my intelligence because
one day I am going to college with this brain!

—Girl, 9, Utah

**I hide it because in fourth grade my friends found
out, and they ditched me. That is the worst feeling a
kid can have.**

**—Boy, 13, Ohio**

In gifted classes, where everyone knows that you're
gifted, no one really cares or thinks about it. Also, I have
a crush on some of the guys in that class, so when I'm
in it, I try to stick out with the fact that I'm gifted.

—Girl, 13, Texas

**Being an accelerant almost ensures you can't hide
giftedness. But, I'm growing and hope to get close in
size to my classmates soon.**

**—Boy, 13, Ohio**

At summer camp I tried. I wanted to see what it was like
to be normal. But, it obviously didn't work since all the
counselors thought I was one of them.

—Girl, 13, Ontario, Canada

**I don't try to hide that I'm gifted, but I don't like the
label. Why can't they just say we are "normal with an
edge"?**

**—Boy, 13, Ohio**

I downplay my abilities at school so expectations don't rise. This gives me mental time to wander through my interests without stressing over worksheets, tests, or projects.

—Girl, 14, Belarus

**Yes, all the time, to fit in. I don't even do extra credit work anymore, and I don't ask if I can work ahead.**

**—Boy, 14, Iowa**

Sometimes, when I'm trying to fit in and have fun, I don't want to show people my differences. I don't push the fact that I'm gifted in other people's faces. That would just turn them off. I usually appear the same as them and wait for them to discover on their own that I might have a gift.

—Girl, 14, Maine

**No, I can't hide who I am. It's something I used to do, and it caused me immense stress. I was always afraid someone would find out that I really liked to read and learn. Since then, I've learned otherwise and am proud of who and what I am.**

**—Boy, 14, Kansas**

Usually, when I'm introduced to a new person, I "lower my intellect" so I don't scare them away. If they come back to talk to me, then I up the intellect.

—Girl, 15, Tennessee

**You cannot camouflage who you are. The pressure builds to explosive internal levels until you have to come out. It's much more tenable to just be yourself. No false pretenses.**

**—Boy, 15, Florida**

Yes, I sometimes hide it. I'm lazy, so if I underachieve, teachers expect less of me and I have a lot more time to do whatever I want, whether that be sports, drawing, or learning about autoimmune diseases.

—Girl, 16, Indiana

Trying to fit in with everyone is highly overrated. Being gifted exposes you to other gifted individuals who will likely become your friends. And real friends are much more important than just being popular.

—Girl, 15, Mississippi

Yes, there have been several times when I won't tell people about my gifted school or me being classified as gifted. The reason is when other kids hear my school's name, the first thing they say is, "He thinks he's better than us" and "He thinks he's all that." Actually, it's just the opposite: I just want to be a kid and just be me.

—Boy, 16, Ohio

I just try to keep my mouth shut. It only makes others dislike me when I speak.

—Girl, 17, South Carolina

# YOUR TURN

**Pro/Con Chart**

Fold a sheet of paper down the center "hot dog bun" style. In one column, write down the positives (pros) about being gifted. List as many as you can in 3 minutes.

Repeat the process, listing the negatives (cons) about being gifted in the other column.

This exercise gives you an indication of your outlook on life as a gifted person:

> More pros than cons? You see the glass of life as half full and have a positive outlook, tending to be hopeful and optimistic.
> More cons than pros? You see the glass of life as half empty and tend to worry what negative things might happen next.

How can you alter your mindset to feel more positive and optimistic?

I do hide my giftedness when meeting new people or entering a new setting. It's always better to be humble and listen to learn before announcing a competition point to others.

—Boy, 17, Iowa

**Maybe I tried to hide it in middle school. But doesn't everyone try to hide who they are in middle school?**
**—Girl, 18, Virginia**

I have, unfortunately, lowered my standards so I do not fall from lofty heights in the eyes of my friends.

—Boy, 18, Tennessee

**I have to in my culture. Girls are expected to do as [they are] told. You cannot outshine boys. I look forward to changing this attitude as I enter adulthood.**
**—Girl, 18, Riyadh, Saudi Arabia**

I avoid telling strangers or casual acquaintances that I go to Yale, since it usually leads to an awkwardly congratulatory conversation about how smart I must be.

—Girl, 19, Connecticut

**It would be hard for me to hide that I'm gifted, because the way I talk and think just screams "gifted"!**
**—Girl, 19, North Carolina**

# FINDING INTERNAL DRIVE

As a teen, life is often like the mystery meat lunch at school. You are not sure what is in it and can't quite place that semifamiliar smell. Every so often, something surfaces that clearly defines the moment. This clarity sometimes lasts for quite a while. Other times it is fleeting.

Up to this point in the chapter, we have been dealing with general ideas and experiences associated with giftedness. We shift here to explore qualities that add to the uniqueness of how you develop.

In this section, we focus on the differences between interests and passions as a way to show how the personal and emotional sides of life impact the choices we make. This is probably something you haven't really thought about, but might help you make a few decisions based on more than what other people expect for you.

Here's what your peers had to say.

> ## Sometimes gifted people talk about intensities or passions rather than interests. What's the difference?

Interests are small, but intensities are what you would consider doing with your life.

—Boy, 13, Ohio

**Interests come and go. Passions stay and overwhelm you.**

**—Girl, 13, New Jersey**

Interests: Fleeting moments of fun. Passions: A virtual train wreck of focus.

—Boy, 14, Texas

**Writing is my absolute passion. History, ancient times, the English language, grammar . . . they are my passions. They are my love. For me, writing is like breathing. It's addictive, and I can't live without it. Interests, on the other hand, are those things that you like to do but you don't hold them within your heart. You**

**don't defend them viciously to anyone who dares to question your love for them. Interests don't make up your life—they supplement it.**

**—Girl, 14, Australia**

The difference between passions and interests? Simple: Semantics and access.

—Boy, 15, Kentucky

**Intensities and passions are things you can't live without. For me, that's music. It makes me happy and it makes me feel whole.**

**—Girl, 15, Texas**

Interests are pursued for entertainment. Passions are doggedly pursued for purpose, either for the betterment of oneself or one's community. Honestly, I think my most profound passion is the search . . . for passion. Most frustrating of all is that among my peers, sometimes I feel alone on this quest.

—Boy, 15, Wisconsin

**Nothing important is accomplished by interest, it is accomplished by passion. It is the gifted person who makes life work for the average person.**

**—Girl, 15, Indiana**

The difference is that interests can be purely academic, while intensities or passions require a sense of personal involvement or care. The distinction is especially important in gifted individuals who are interested in just about anything.

—Boy, 15, Maine

**I am definitely a person with passions (obsessions, really). I have gone through so many obsessions: fairies, dinosaurs, cats, prehistoric humans, ants, and now, anime and manga. With a passion, you want to immerse yourself in it, learn everything about it, read all the books you can. You want to know what it's like**

to be a fairy, a dinosaur, a cat, a whatever. You want to live it.

—Girl, 15, Illinois

I had interests as a preteen. Now my life is ruled by passions (and hormones).

—Boy, 15, Oregon

The difference is what motivates you. For instance, I was interested to answer these questions through sheer force of curiosity (one of my strongest emotions), and it was fun. My opinions rarely matter, and I doubt that this will ever be read by many people, if anyone at all, but I wanted to answer them anyway. As far as a passion goes, I have no idea yet, since I've never had one, so the blind man isn't going to try calling the sun green.

—Boy, 16, Iowa

Interests come and go, like boyfriends and girlfriends, but passions last forever, and they leave an imprint on you.

—Girl, 16, Colorado

Petulant purveyors of projected attention—Passions. Insufficient interludes of intrigue and wonder—Interests.

—Boy, 16, Kansas

Passions are deep-seated emotions that drive you beyond your intellectual comfort level. They define your life, like it or not.

—Girl, 17, New York

You get totally absorbed by your passions. You think about them at school, after school, when you're trying to sleep, and when you wake up in the morning. Your world is centered around them, and you try to make whatever you can relate to them. I am currently passionless and have been for a while. This makes me feel depressed and, to some extent, like my life lacks meaning.

—Boy, 17, Kansas

Interests are primordial buds of passions. Some are lost to natural selection. Others are lost to unfortunate events. Passions are the few that remain as we age. They blossom into beautiful signposts pointing direction in our lives.

—Girl, 18, New Mexico

**Passions are your life's determined path. Interests are all the possibilities available until you choose to sink your teeth in. These become the passions.**

—**Boy, 18, Oklahoma**

Passions drive a person. Interests are just an escape from serious things. They are more for entertainment and release than passions are.

—Girl, 19, Oklahoma

**A passion is something you love to do your best at, while an interest is something you like to have fun with. It's good to have both in life, but know the difference. Don't let an interest take away your passion, because passions last longer and are closer to your heart.**

—**Girl, 19, Pennsylvania**

# YOUR TURN

**A Letter to Yourself**

Think about a passion in your own life. How long have you held this passion? How did it start for you? Do you see yourself continuing to pursue this passion as you grow older, or can you imagine other passions taking over?

Write about this passion in detail. Then, put a copy of your writing into an envelope, seal it, and date it. Put the envelope away, and don't open it for one year. When you do open it, you may be surprised at what you read.

This chapter addressed one of the most frustrating aspects of being a gifted individual—understanding what the label means. You saw that there are myriad ways to describe giftedness, and often—like beauty—it exists in the eyes of the beholder.

Will experts in the field come to a consensus on the definition of giftedness? It is doubtful. But, more importantly, a single definition would limit recognition of unique traits in individuals.

Our take is that giftedness is a benchmark category. It does not conclusively define differences that should separate individuals. It is a verification that some individuals display tendencies, behaviors, and abilities that warrant support in order to develop fully. Yet, this support does not guarantee an outcome in caliber of performance that is exquisite or exceptional.

This is an area that many people overlook or do not understand. Services for the gifted will be discussed and explored in subsequent chapters. Here, we begin with the statement that giftedness is a state of being and becoming. It is who you are—regardless of measurement—and our goal is to provide a way for you to invest in yourself while gaining awareness that who you are is as, if not more, important than what you can do.

You might have talents, interests, and passions, but without a cause that deeply affects your sense of self, there is no feeling of connectedness or accomplishment. The developing you is unique and highly capable. Let's explore this further.

# chapter 2

# FRIENDS, PEERS, AND FITTING IN

ONE of the benefits of growing up gifted is finding you can fit into many social contexts.

Huh?

What we mean is this: If you are a 14-year old with the vocabulary of an adult, the interests of a "typical" teenager, and the sophistication to know the difference between irony and nuance, you can get along with kids your age, older teens who appreciate your maturity, and adults who talk *with* you, not *at* you. And, should you be so lucky as to also appreciate good fart jokes, you'll get along with younger kids, too.

That's not to say that traversing the social waters is always easy for gifted teens. Sometimes, you may feel that you don't quite fit into conversations about topics that absorb the lives of others your age but that bore you to tears (does it *really* matter who dates whom in eighth grade?). Or, you may feel slighted when an older teen or adult with whom you've been interacting suddenly decides you are "too young" for a particular event or conversation. When your body says "I'm 14," your mind shouts "I think like a 20-year-old," and your musical interests range from Death Cab for Cutie to Debussy, figuring out who you should be at any given moment can be a challenge.

In this chapter, we're hoping that the comments made by gifted teens like (or unlike) you can put this social situation into perspective. Is it OK to conform—to go along with the crowd—or is it better to stand your ground as the individual you are? Do you lower your vocabulary to get understood by classmates, or do you believe it is their task to rise to your level of talk? Can you be gifted and a teenager, too, when it comes to getting along with those around you? As you might expect, there is not a "one-choice-fits-all" answer to any of these questions, yet we hope that by reading the thoughts and suggestions of other gifted teens, you might come to see that the range of options before you is pretty broad.

## How do friends react to your abilities? What do friends do or say that makes you feel good or bad about being gifted?

My friends see me as one of the guys, only a lot smarter and with a bigger vocabulary.
—Boy, 13, New Jersey

I surround myself with other people who are smart. We all try to push each other forward, with interesting science literature and political debates at the lunch table. There's a plethora of inside jokes that encourage our individual passions. Our lunch table bursts out laughing at any mention of the words "mononucleosis," "tourism," or "socioeconomic." We're in this together.
—Girl, 13, New Jersey

People I know at school are jealous of my grades and how I am able to skim by in my classes and still make the honor roll. Despite my all-out efforts to be friendly to everyone and to "fit in" with the norm, many people brand me as a "soce" or a "teacher's pet"—both a cross between a goody-two-shoes and a know-it-all.

—Girl, 13, Wyoming

**My friends treat me different just because I'm in a gifted program. They like saying rude and dumb jokes about my abilities. No one should get made fun of just because they are smart.**

**—Boy, 14, Texas**

I try not to let the fact that people think I am gifted affect my social life. I want to be like my friends, just another person, because being different sets you apart. Anyone who is different gets laughed at.

—Girl, 14, Oklahoma

**Sometimes, a phone call that begins "Hi, can you explain the science homework?" leaves me feeling like I have a big sign on my back claiming that I don't want friends, just questions.**

**—Girl, 14, Massachusetts**

[Because] I have been in college since I was 12, my classmates either ignore me or are very nice. No one has been unkind to me since I started at the university. Over the past 3 years, I have almost started believing again that people can be nice.

—Boy, 15, North Carolina

**For the past 8 years, I have been trying to make people understand that I have the same kinds of feelings and needs as other kids my age. Yet, people continue to think I am "beyond that."**

**—Girl, 15, Kansas**

## YOUR TURN

Into which of the aforementioned camps do you fall? The one that espouses exposing your intelligence for all to see, or the one that eschews such discussions at all costs? See if you can figure out which situations you find most accepting of your giftedness, and those where you believe it is better to keep your intelligence hidden from others. Can you see any trends in your answers? For instance, are there certain groups where you know you cannot and will not share your giftedness? Do you shine in some settings but not others?

Most of the people I consider friends are from Internet chat rooms. It is one of the few places where the jokes and chat go fast enough to keep me interested.
—Boy, 16, Virginia

**I don't like it when my friends say, "You did an awesome job!" when I put 5% effort into my work.**
**—Boy, 16, Indiana**

Most of my friends don't care one way or the other about my giftedness. When I was younger and had imaginary friends, if one of them started making fun of me, I'd just get rid of him.

—Boy, 16, Tennessee

**People make fun of you when your intelligence exceeds theirs because people fear what they do not understand.**

**—Boy, 16, California**

All of my friends are incredibly gifted themselves. We hang out at a coffee shop drinking iced tea, discussing philosophy, and playing bridge. This isn't elitism, it's just who we relate to.

—Boy, 17, Virginia

**When I'm around other gifted people, it's a totally different atmosphere that really lifts me up.**
**—Girl, 19, New York**

Several responses in this section reveal how readily some teens are willing to admit their giftedness, while others speak of their intelligence gingerly, tiptoeing around the topic to avoid a head-on collision with others who demean or dismiss intellectual talents. We find ourselves caught up in this same situation when dealing with individuals in our lives. (So, don't think this is something you will just outgrow when you become an adult!) But, it is important to gain perspective in life—and take calculated chances in order to grow.

## Do you ever do anything just to go along with the crowd? Why or why not?

No, if being dumb or acting dumb makes you fit in better, then I'd rather not fit in at all.
—Boy, 13, Georgia

**Mostly, I am the one that comes up with the ideas, so I am the crowd leader. A lot of people look up to me.**
**—Boy, 13, California**

If you really knew anything about middle school social politics, you wouldn't want to go along with the crowd.
—Girl, 13, Ontario

**Yes, I have done things just to go along with the crowd before, because I was tired of being "so special" . . . and so alone. I just wanted to belong to the big crowd for a while. (It never worked very well, though.)**
**—Girl, 13, Maine**

I guess everyone has to do a certain amount of camouflage just to get by in high school. I don't go along with the crowd so much as I disguise my speech so that I sound somewhat normal (i.e., incoherent). You have

# YOUR TURN

**Friends and Acquaintances: Discovering the Difference**

Complete an inventory of the people you would call friends and see if you can figure out what you enjoy about your top three relationships. Also, if you have any so-called "friends" who connect with you only when they need help with getting a high grade on a project or test (or otherwise need you for something), come up with a plan to change the dynamics of this situation. Can you think of ways to diplomatically let these acquaintances know that you are on to their game?

to camouflage yourself a little for self-protection.
—Girl, 14, Utah

**Nope, because I don't have the proper social skills to know what "the crowd" wants.**
**—Boy, 14, Massachusetts**

I wish I was invited to parties and, if I were, I might do something considered "irresponsibly adolescent." I sometimes tell my parents that I wish I were an underachieving delinquent, so that when I make a mistake or do something unethical it wouldn't be such a big deal.
—Girl, 15, Indiana

**No, I've learned it's better to do things for myself. If other people want to jump off a bridge, I hope they have fun.**
**—Boy, 15, Texas**

When I was younger, I wanted so much to be liked and accepted. Then, as I got older, I realized that I don't want to be like "those people" at all. I am my own person. I speak my opinion. I wear what I want to wear, and I say what I believe. That doesn't mean my life is any easier or that I've suddenly found my place in the world, but I feel better about me.
—Girl, 15, Kansas

. . . sometimes I do because I'm lonely. I need to pretend I like something so I can feel that I have something in common with my friends.

—Girl, 16, Pennsylvania

Yeah, I do. You can't just sit back and be stubborn about your beliefs. Adaptation is a part of life.

—Boy, 16, Texas

If I do something to go along with the crowd, it's a carefully considered decision that I make on a case-by-case basis.

—Boy, 17, Nebraska

I'm just wallpaper. I try not to stick out because, as the ancient Asian saying goes, "The nail that sticks out gets hammered down."

—Girl, 17, New York

Sometimes, "dumbing down" is a misnomer for a life skill strategy. It is time to recognize how "smart" it is to adjust your communication style to your audience in order to socialize.

—Girl, 17, Minnesota

I found that getting into college allowed me to "reboot" myself. I could blend in easily without having the stigma of being one of the gifted kids hanging over my head. I found that just being me was good enough. And, I found that there were lots of other kids who didn't say anything about being gifted, but did have some of the same quirks and interests that I had. It was finally nice to be someplace that I fit in without having to try to fit in.

—Boy, 18, Virginia

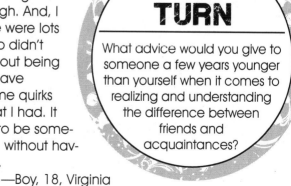

**YOUR TURN**

What advice would you give to someone a few years younger than yourself when it comes to realizing and understanding the difference between friends and acquaintances?

**Not in elementary or middle school, but in high school, I became more concerned about social acceptance, but not to the extent that I would do things against my morals.**
                                        **—Girl, 19, Connecticut**

Many of the comments in this section allude to the notion that friendships are formed (and kept) for different reasons. Maybe some of your friends are as smart as you or smarter, and their intellects entertain you, making them fun to be around—sometimes. Other friends may be less capable intellectually, yet you get along because of common interests or a long history of good times spent together since you were 4 years old.

Another side of friendship is understanding that not everyone is a friend. Sometimes others are friendly because they need or want something rather than just accepting you as you are. It is these situations that cause angst for many gifted teens, who want to fit in, but also realize that being taken advantage of isn't high on the list of positive life experiences.

In the section that follows, we focus on subtle differences that gifted individuals feel and face when interacting with others. There are differences in giftedness and gifted people. Very few individuals who have been formally identified are "practically perfect in every way" (as Mary Poppins liked to say). Does it take more mental energy on your part to be intelligent and show it or to "plead ignorance" and keep your smarts to yourself? Let's see what others have said.

## What is it like when you feel smarter than some of your friends?

Sometimes I wish I was just a normal kid, one who liked to hang out with other girls, who thought that dressing in something fashionable and being well-liked was almost as important as getting good grades. I'd like to live just one day to see what living that life would be like.

—Girl, 13, Texas

**I don't always know how to handle my giftedness around my friends. Who should I tell? Who shouldn't I tell? When am I bragging, and when am I just telling the truth?**

**—Boy, 13, Nebraska**

It gets aggravating having to explain a joke to my friends more than once. By then, all the fun has gone out of it.

—Boy, 13, Florida

**Being gifted doesn't change the fact that I'm still a normal kid, and actually, sometimes I can be quite stupid.**

**—Boy, 14, Utah**

It's hard when I see my friends make mistakes that I wouldn't make and then start to automatically correct them. I have to tell myself, "They're not like you. They don't know what you know. Let them learn in their own way." Can I please express how utterly frustrating this is?

—Girl, 14, Australia

**Thus far in high school, I have made friends with more juniors and seniors than freshmen because we are closer to the same thought and maturity levels.**

**—Boy, 14, Ohio**

When I was younger, it was very frustrating for me to interact with kids my own age because it seemed like they were from another planet. They acted like babies to me. My teachers used to tell me not to use words the other students couldn't understand. I can only hope that my giftedness will pay off in whatever career I choose after college.

—Girl, 15, Indiana

# BIG BANG, INDEED!

Mayim Bialik, who plays a neurobiologist on the sitcom "The Big Bang Theory," isn't stretching too far in playing her character. In real life, Mayim is actually Dr. Bialik, as she has a Ph.D. in neuroscience. As she told *Parade* magazine, "I can . . . recreationally psychoanalyze our staff so I know what personality quirks to expect!" ("Mayim Bialik's Braniac Advantage," October 2011)

**Sometimes I feel like I make others think that I am smarter than they are when I don't mean to portray that idea at all. I intimidate them when I don't mean to.**

**—Girl, 16, Minnesota**

A lot of times, my age peers can be really shallow and immature. I just try to remind myself that they're at a different place than I am, mentally and developmentally. I have fun with them at their level, but I feel unfulfilled a lot when there is nobody at my level to relate to.

—Boy, 17, Kansas

**It all kinda evens out sooner or later. By high school, some friends are smarter, some friends are not as smart, and you develop different areas of expertise. Being smarter than my friends is not how I think about us at all.**

**—Girl, 18, Kentucky**

Many gifted students mistakenly believe that if others do not have their knowledge they are somehow "lesser." An artist does not know the musical repertoire of a pianist, and neither may know the plays of a football jock, but I have personally been in the same math class with all three types. That's life, isn't it?

—Boy, 19, Tennessee

## YOUR TURN

What are some possible reasons that teachers, counselors, or other students may think that gifted people have an undeserved superiority complex (more commonly known as elitism)? Examine your own life circumstances and note if there have been times when you mistook being "better at" something for being "better than" someone else.

Several respondents in this section mentioned that being intelligent does not make you intrinsically better than others who are not as smart. This is so true, yet it seems to be a continuing problem with some people (gifted and otherwise) who assume that you think you are more worthy as a person because you are more intelligent.

Take time to complete the Your Turn activity for this section. It will enlighten you to perceived elitism that others might hold about giftedness and expose ways you might be unwittingly contributing to the perceptions that other people hold.

# PEERS AND PEER GROUPS

Many times, the word "peer" is misused, as it is often considered a synonym for "age mate." Thus, if you are 15 years old, many adults assume that your "peer group," likewise, is composed of other 15-year-olds. In examining your own life, do you find that you use chronological age as a major or minor criterion for selecting friends? Do you have "peers" who are several years older or younger than you are? If age is not the most important determinant for choosing friendships, what other criteria do you use? And how can you convince adults who worry about your relationships with people older or younger than you that you are perfectly safe and sane in seeking out these individuals? The comments that follow might help you develop some answers to these intriguing questions.

## How are you the same as and different than other people your age?

I think the biggest thing I have in common with other children my age is that adults only take me seriously when it is convenient to do so. Sometimes it's hard to talk with other kids my age, because I find myself jumping from Harry Potter to telekinesis to quantum physics, for I find that every subject presents 20 tangents to go out on. I imagine that's hard for other kids to keep track of.

—Girl, 13, Pennsylvania

I am a 13-year-old girl. I talk about guys, clothes, fashion. But not on a superficial level. Guys are my best friends, clothes are made to keep us comfortable, and fashion is nonexistent. And people wonder why we don't always fit in . . .

—Girl, 13, Ontario

I think that my "peers" don't use their brains too much. They don't seem very curious about the world and are not interested in pursuing further investigation on topics discussed in school. For example, they don't care about philology, yet after watching *The Fellowship of the Ring*, I found some websites and started learning Sindarin Elvish.

—Girl, 14, New Jersey

**I am different from other kids my age in many ways. For example, I can hold a conversation with an adult over anything interesting. They can't.**

**—Boy, 14, Indiana**

I think I am a little too pensive, too intense, for some people.

—Girl, 14, Wisconsin

**I am on the brink of independence and struggling with my place in the world, just as my classmates are, even if we cope with it in different ways. In short, we are adolescents and as such, must bind together since the rest of society has just cause to avoid us.**

**—Boy, 15, Massachusetts**

I enjoy playing a lot of sports, and I feel there are stereotypes against kids who are considered gifted. When someone thinks of a gifted person, most kids imagine them to be geeky, having no social life, and not doing anything other than schoolwork. I blame a lot of this on how the media portray gifted kids in movies and TV shows. Personally, I have met many people who are not only gifted, but they are great athletes, musicians, and all-around people.

—Boy, 15, Florida

**One thing that sets me apart from my peers is motivation. Many of the kids around me simply don't care about the future. I, however, know that I want to succeed, and I have plans on how to achieve my goals.**

**Also, I tend to appreciate the arts and literature more than others my age. I love watching plays and old movies, whereas most kids my age get bored.**
—**Girl, 16, Michigan**

I have found that I do tend to think more outside the box and ask more complex questions than many people in my classes. This can come as a disadvantage, because the benefits of an intellectual discussion are lost among these people.
—Boy, 16, Ohio

**It is hard to have an interesting conversation with most of my classmates, because they say I don't make sense. But with my gifted friends, they finish my sentences on the same subject.**
—**Girl, 16, Iowa**

I am mostly different, because I think most people my age are shallow and worry about themselves when there is so much famine and war and other important things to consider in life. In school, I do not participate in some classes, because the students are so uninformed.
—Boy, 16, California

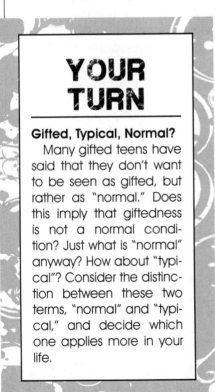

## YOUR TURN

**Gifted, Typical, Normal?**
Many gifted teens have said that they don't want to be seen as gifted, but rather as "normal." Does this imply that giftedness is not a normal condition? Just what is "normal" anyway? How about "typical"? Consider the distinction between these two terms, "normal" and "typical," and decide which one applies more in your life.

**All of my friends are incredibly smart, and I just don't associate with average kids. It's not any sort of elitism, we just don't have anything in common. I want to discuss philosophy, whereas they want to discuss MTV. Not a whole lot of crossover . . .**
—**Boy, 17, Virginia**

Well, I'm mostly the same in that I like the same clothes, clubbing, rock music, boys, and the rest of that teenage folderol. Sometimes, though, I feel I'm seen as a poser or nerd, in lieu of the cool kid whose persona I affect. My friends tell me I need to chill out, that I am paranoid. It's a feeling I can't shake—the feeling of being a stranger in a strange land.

—Girl, 17, New York

**I am a teenager before I am gifted, so while I understand certain things at a higher level than the normal student, I am still experiencing many things in the same ways as my friends. I am still going through the late stages of puberty, my mind is still maturing as well as learning, and I still lack many of the skills I shall need for college and beyond. In fact, some of my friends have already taken positions on adult issues like religion, sexuality, and government that I lack.**

**—Boy, 18, Tennessee**

I tended (and tend) to be more introverted, more thoughtful, and often more cynical than most kids my age. Other than that, though, I was always a "normal" kid. I think people forget that even if someone is labeled gifted, they're still a kid.

—Girl, 19, North Carolina

In 1917, Barry Commoner wrote that the First Law of Ecology is that "everything is connected to everything else." Well, what is true in ecology is also true in the daily lives we lead: Decisions have consequences, which lead to more decisions that have *further* consequences. In the essay that follows, Jo Riemann learned early on about the interconnectedness of the many parts of herself—her intellectual life, her social life, her interests and ambitions. She admits to not always handling particular situations with grace or good judgment, but along the way, she learned just how important it is to be able to look yourself in the mirror, to face both your virtues and your vices, and to grow from there.

# Jo Riemann
## Finding Yourself

Some people who are interested in mathematics join the school math team. I live and breathe mathematics and went through much of an undergraduate and master's curriculum in 2 years of independent learning. It's literally the language through which I understand the relationships in the world around me—power laws governing tree branching, knot theory in a tied shoelace . . . The alacrity with which I learn or investigate mathematics (or science in general, philosophy, machine learning, or literature) revs me with energy, and I connect whatever I happen to be studying with many other domains of study.

I knew that I was different upon entering kindergarten, as other children didn't seem to enjoy using toys for physics experiments. Many teachers regarded my differences as oddities or aberrations needing to be fixed, and some in the earliest years went so far as to punish me when I couldn't figure out how to be a "normal" kid (such as not understanding that I was to stay in the children's section during library time when my parents had let me venture to the adult section for quite some time). Many expected me to be perfect all the time in everything that I did, and most of my childhood consisted of floundering in my attempts to imitate my classmates and others my age.

This continued through childhood, and my parents scrambled to provide outside opportunities and even transferred me to another school in search of a better fit. In early adolescence, I found a solution that would destroy my differences—make me apathetic toward school and injustice, constrain the way I saw material and played with ideas that were expected of intelligent students (no leaping ahead in material, questioning lessons, or going more in depth on assignments), and numb the pain of bullying and being misunderstood—I started drinking and using drugs. Thus began the on-again, off-again nightmare solution through the remainder of my teen years.

When I turned 15, I was finally old enough to radically accelerate (and take classes with my group of older friends) and take advantage of academic opportunities away from home. However, I eventually couldn't take advantage of this newfound access to academia, as it became harder and harder to quit partying.

During my first year of college, one counselor asked about the scores I had achieved on the SAT and ACT as a preteen (higher than the 50% level for seniors in my weakest area and higher than the 90% level for seniors in my areas of strength). This addressed my giftedness and what it meant, which I attributed to my interactions with people and the world as a whole. No one had ever linked my abilities with my experiences.

As a part of my recovery, I took an inventory of myself, including my intellectual part, and learned to accept it for what it is—neither inherently good, nor bad. Rather, how I use it determines whether it is an asset or a liability.

It allows me to delve deeply into spiritual exploration and has provided me with many opportunities to be of service. I've been able to use my experiences to change legislation and school policies via several advocacy groups and, through my research, which ties together many different fields of interest, focus on entangling the inner workings of HIV and factors influencing mental health with the hope of informing policy and developing more efficacious interventions.

Looking back on my experiences, I wish I had been able to discover and discuss my giftedness and its relationship to my schooling experiences, especially with respect to the notion that there was something about me that needed "fixing," with someone knowledgeable about levels and areas of giftedness earlier in my life. My family and teachers didn't have much information about this when I was growing up, but, these days, there are wonderful resources and advocacy groups online for students, parents, and educators (such as the Hoagies Gifted website and the Davidson Institute). Discussing this may have helped me better understand my differences in the context of school and children my age. Differences don't have to be negative; armed with knowledge and the support of adults around you, you can use this difference to follow your passions to places beyond your dreams.

*Jo Riemann, 24, is a medical statistician and author living in the southern United States who is passionate about educational policy and legislation to help gifted students. She hopes her candid story helps other young people avoid some of the difficulties she experienced as a young person.*

There are many stereotypes about gifted teens—that they are nerdy, unathletic, and endlessly hopeless when it comes to fashion, music, and (as one respondent put it) "the rest of that teenage folderol." Do you believe any of these stereotypes are actually true, and if so, which ones? Look around you: In your school, what is the overall impression of teachers, administrators, and other students about gifted kids? Are there any stereotypes that are obvious? Subtle? Or, is giftedness just one of many characteristics that some kids have and some kids don't have, so it's not looked at as any big deal?

# SUMMARY

This chapter could have been titled "Choose Wisely: It's Your Life." But, as factual as that title might be, we felt the need to provide a bit of a road map for you to consider. Best of all, the road map comes from your peers—other gifted teens facing similar concerns and questions, with an enduring optimism that the future is a smorgasbord of opportunities.

Beware, though. There are choices that can lead to unforeseen issues and outcomes. No one has ever said that being gifted means you will always make the right decision and everything will turn out grand. The world can be a pretty harsh place—no matter how rosy your glasses seem to picture it!

Overall, though, you have ultimate control over your developing self. If you find yourself currently "down in the dumps," reach out to a trusted friend, parent, teacher, or school counselor. There are many of us here for you who are ready and willing to help.

Take stock of where you currently stand or what reality seems to mean to you at this point in life. And look to the future. You have ample opportunity to steer a path based on your sense of being and becoming. The journey might follow the path of least resistance or require you to blaze trails through unexplored territory. From our experience, the journey will likely be filled with both approaches as time winds on. The key to everything? Keep your dreams alive. The next chapter will help fortify you on this journey.

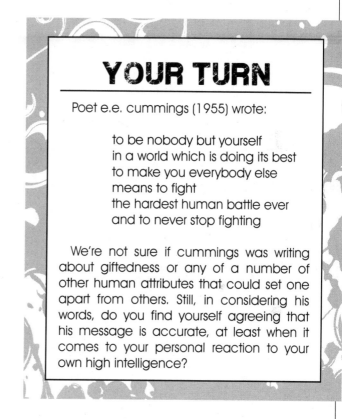

# YOUR TURN

Poet e.e. cummings (1955) wrote:

> to be nobody but yourself
> in a world which is doing its best
> to make you everybody else
> means to fight
> the hardest human battle ever
> and to never stop fighting

We're not sure if cummings was writing about giftedness or any of a number of other human attributes that could set one apart from others. Still, in considering his words, do you find yourself agreeing that his message is accurate, at least when it comes to your personal reaction to your own high intelligence?

# chapter 3

# WHAT DO YOU EXPECT?

**THE** long-suffering *Peanuts* cartoon character Charlie Brown was lamenting yet another life disappointment when he spoke the following words: "There is no heavier burden than a great potential." We're not sure if Charlie Brown qualified as gifted in his school, but his lament over not meeting up to expectations—his own or someone else's—is a sentiment shared by many capable people.

*Potential*: It's a word to love, it's a word to hate. The positive part about having a lot of potential is that people often praise your capabilities and achievements and extol the wonders of how far you will go in life by saying things like, "You can be anything you want to be when you grow up" or "That fine mind of yours is a great gift—use it well." The negative part of having a lot of potential is that no two people seem to agree on how high your potential really is or whether or not you are taking full advantage of it. So, if you get a B– on the world's toughest precalculus test, a comment like "I expected more from someone with your abilities" might be heard. And, if your career goal is to be a CG artist in an up-and-coming gaming company, you might hear that you are "wasting your potential" by not choosing a more, shall we say, *gifted* occupation like law, engineering, or medicine.

In our work with gifted students, we have found that academic expectations are sometimes so high that anything less than an A+ is considered a failure, either by some adult in your life—a parent, teacher, or high school counselor—or by the person you look at in the mirror each day. "How high is *high enough*?" "How good is *good enough*?" These are questions that gifted students often struggle with as they try to maneuver the often rocky waters of life expectations.

The comments in this chapter will help you examine the importance (or lack thereof) that you place on success, however it is measured. Moreover, the reflective nature of many of these comments may help you to see personal accomplishment (or lack thereof) through a lens that is tethered less to *grades* and more to *growth*.

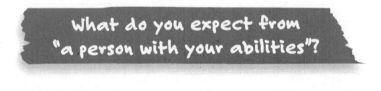

### What do you expect from "a person with your abilities"?

I expect to have very ambitious dreams and to try to be somebody who can affect the world in a good way.
—Boy, 13, Iowa

**Being gifted may be a blessing and all, but gifted students and adults have their off days, too. Even if we're up and running most of the time, we all need a break once in a while.**
—Girl, 13, Nebraska

In terms of pure expectations, I expect someone with my abilities to be more introspective and studious, although I know that isn't always the case. I expect deep interest in several areas and a bit of idealism.

—Girl, 14, Massachusetts

**The ability to correct actions before they become issues. This is what I expect from a person with my abilities, but it isn't what I do myself. For some reason, I just forget things and issues sneak up and snowball on me. My parents say it's because I'm a teen. I worry that I might not be gifted anymore.**

**—Boy, 14, Michigan**

I don't expect anything from a "person with my abilities." If people are smart, and they choose not to use their abilities, then so be it. People should be allowed to make their own decisions and not be pressured into doing something they don't want to do just because they are "smart."

—Girl, 15, Utah

**I expect this person to be self-sufficient, confident, and cool under pressure. I expect them to always have answers or to be able to deflect questions that are confusing. I expect them to keep everyone on their toes and to be wildly successful and creative. Boy that's a lot to live up to, but that's what I expect.**

**—Boy, 15, Illinois**

I expect to fulfill my potential . . . but I don't know what that is yet, because my choices are unlimited.

—Boy, 16, California

**I expect to reach for the stars and keep my feet on the ground. I want to do great things and contribute to society in many ways. I expect to be [well off], but also give back to others.**

**—Girl, 16, Louisiana**

I expect to develop my abilities. I expect to think hard and deeply about things. I expect to feel some sense of loneliness and isolation.

—Boy, 17, Kansas

**Nothing other than finding happiness in life by living life according to his or her wishes and dreams, not listening to and being judged by trying to please other people. There is too much pressure on people with abilities like mine to live up to expectations of others. Life is for living on your own terms, not to be done through decisions and expectations made by other people for you.**

**—Girl, 17, Florida**

I expect them to grow up with lots of dreams only to watch them drop by the wayside one by one as decisions are made that close life in on a narrow path. This might sound depressing but it is the reality the gifted face as the realization that working within society requires personal sacrifices. You have to choose and live with those choices.

—Boy, 18, Massachusetts

**I stopped expecting anything as I met more and more gifted people. There's a whole range of them out there, who cover the entire spectrum on just about any topic you can come up with. In essence, we're all just people.**

**—Girl, 19, Kansas**

# YOUR TURN

Although most decisions are best made when you put in some time thinking about your possible options, there is something to be said for answering some things off the top of your head—things like this activity. Read through the following sentence stems and complete the sentence with the first thought that comes into your mind. Why your first thought? Because it is generally the most honest, unfiltered response. Once you've completed the sentences below, share your list with someone else who has completed this activity, and talk over any items that you find interesting or thought provoking.

➤ When I get an A in school, _____

➤ When I *don't* get an A in school, _____

➤ Most of my friends expect me _____

➤ I expect myself _____

➤ When I hear the word "gifted," I think_____

➤ The biggest misconception others have of being gifted is _____
_____

➤ If I could convince my teachers of one thing,_____
_____

➤ I do best in school when _____

➤ My social life _____

➤ When I consider my future, _____

➤ The best part about being gifted is _____

➤ The worst part about being gifted is _____

➤ If I could change one thing about my life,_____
_____

➤ If I could change one thing about our world, _____
_____

One of the hardest things about growing up gifted is that in those times when you *don't* act gifted, everyone seems to notice. So, when that errant B+ shows its ugly face on your report card, or you forget to feed the cat for the third time in a week, people around you give you these funny looks that say loudly and clearly, "Gifted? Not so much today."

August's essay on the following page is a tribute to a few things many gifted people fear most: letting others down, being less than perfect, and not having a plan that'll guide the rest of your life. Then, she provides you with some necessary ammunition to combat these gnawing enemies of self-worth. Learning early in life that when others put you on a pedestal, the only direction to go from there is down, August invites you to do a little bit of inner probing to determine who you are, what really matters, and how *you* define success. And even if she doesn't quote him, August seems to believe in the truth of this line by Oscar Wilde: "Be yourself. Everyone else is taken."

# August Siena Thomas
## After the Applause

Two months after my 18th birthday, I graduated from college. The applause in my university football stadium was deafening, as I stood onstage in my pigtails and my cap and gown.

And then, as all applause must do, it died away. The graduation robes were hung up in my messy closet, the tasseled cap transferred to the enormous fuzzy head of the stuffed gorilla who lives atop my wardrobe.

And what remained? Well, me. Me in my pigtails, standing on a vast heap of scary questions. What was I supposed to do now?

I'd been taking college courses since I was 11. I was good at being a "bright kid," a shiny ball of potential. And yet, *I* knew I *wasn't* just that bright kid anymore. I could no longer base my identity on being "the youngest." I was a college graduate and a legal adult, though still a teenager. I was staring across the bridge from a precocious childhood to whatever might come next.

And boy, was I scared.

This reaction baffled almost everyone I confided in, from my pediatrician to my meditation instructor. "A year out quickly becomes 5!" admonished a professor when I mentioned plans for a gap year. No one but my mother and my very closest friends could understand what I felt.

And yet there was nothing extraordinary in my response. I was barely 18. I knew for certain that I wasn't ready for a doctorate yet, no matter how good my grades were. The thought of plunging into the 9 to 5 routine of an office job was abhorrent. I wanted to keep learning, but not necessarily in school. I wanted to explore. To start trying to grow up (but maybe not too fast). To write and learn new languages and travel. In short, to stretch my wings.

So from age 18 to 20, that's exactly what I've done.

I started driver's ed at age 19. I was the oldest person in my class and had exactly zero talent behind the wheel. At first, it freaked me out—I was supposed to be The Youngest! The Best!

And then, my mother taught me the magic words: *Who cares?*

I stopped feeling embarrassed, got over myself, and got my license.

I learned to teach: little kids, senior citizens, a college course, 450 lively high schoolers. Suddenly I realized just how silly I'd been all those years, worrying what my professors would think of me if I had a quiet day in class, or didn't know the answer to every question. It is very liberating to realize that almost no one's really paying as much attention to you as you think they are (or as you are paying to yourself).

Now, as the anxious clouds started to thin, I began to understand that I was not my resume or my GPA. My life was not a performance for the benefit of others. (My mother, bless her, had been saying this all along, but I hadn't let myself believe it.) My radical acceleration did not define me. It was a biographical fact—the big, splashy, first number with the tap-dancing elephants, not the whole show. (And honestly, how long do you want to watch elephants tap dancing?)

I felt my center of gravity begin to shift slowly, a little uncomfortably, from the cozy, confining past—my life as a bright little kid—to the present.

The present was a very pleasant one. I studied abroad three times. I mastered a new language. I became more relaxed, friendlier, more confident, and less anxious to please. But still I worried. Often. I'd defined myself in terms of external achievements for an awfully long time. Sure, I was fine for the moment. Sure, I knew I needed to take this space as much as I needed anything. But was I destroying myself professionally and academically? What about The Rest of My Life? I mean, I hadn't won an award for weeks and weeks and *weeks*!

I scoured the websites of doctoral programs and fellowships, searching almost desperately. Nothing felt right. There was a very good reason for that: I still wasn't ready. I still needed time. Fortunately, I had it.

I also had a promise to keep. Years ago, I had started a novel. It was time to make it as good as I could, to finally finish it. It can be tough, even frightening, to step off the path of least resistance and make a serious effort to achieve your dreams, especially if those dreams don't come with a blueprint. By dreams I mean what you *actually* want, not the PR you concoct for application essays. Me? I wanted to be a writer; I'd been saying so for years. Now I had to actually face the uncertainty, go from potential to the real deal. Take the risk. So every morning, I get up and that is what I do. That is where my heart is. It matters more to me than any A+ ever will or could.

I'm not half old enough to start dispensing sage advice, but there is one thing I very much want to say to you.

Please, in honor of all of the hard work (yours and everybody else's) that it has taken to get you this far, be courageous. Be true. Commit yourself to the passion that makes you exhilarated, that you *want* to stick with even when you're frustrated and bored. The thing that means so much to you, you'd do if nobody ever gave you an A. If you don't know what it is, that's completely fine. But for heaven's sake, give yourself the space you need to start finding out! You have the time.

What's that? OK, I'll take off the big fake gray beard now. But think about it.

P.S. I turn 21 in a few weeks. I'm a finalist for a Fulbright scholarship, and I've been accepted to a master's program with a wonderful scholarship. And it feels right. Because, at last, I'm ready. For one next step. Not a whole life laid out before me. Just one next step. Who knows what comes after that?

*August Siena Thomas, 20, is a writer based in New England. She graduated from the University of Massachusetts at 18 with two bachelor's degrees. A Davidson Fellow and former Young Scholar, she loves illustrating, traveling, learning languages, and leading online seminars for profoundly gifted kids through the Davidson Institute. She begins her graduate studies in Fall 2012.*

The following section revisits ideas from Chapter 2 to some degree. However, this bit of redundancy reinforces the notion that there are many externally imposed expectations that hinder gifted individuals through no fault of their own. Society holds thoughts and beliefs about every stereotypical group—including the gifted—that should be "flagged for illegal procedure." Unfortunately, there aren't many life referees available with the authority to send offenders to the penalty box (nor is there a penalty box big enough to accommodate all who should serve time there).

Many of these biases and beliefs are off the mark, as we have and will continue to show in this book. But, through their subtle inclusion in people's minds, these expectations cause conflict for individuals trying to understand what being gifted is all about.

What do others—adults or friends—expect from you?

My friends expect me to play with them and do the sorts of things 13-year-old kids do. They do not expect me to want to read books or do math problems all day (and night). Thank goodness!

—Boy, 13, Maryland

**Often, people expect me to be super organized, which I'm not. (Sometimes organization is the bane of discovery.)**

**—Girl, 13, Pennsylvania**

My mom and dad are just Mom and Dad. They're proud when I'm successful and encouraging when I fail. My teachers expect me to be full of ideas when I enter their classrooms.

—Girl, 14, Florida

**Most people expect way too much. They ask for a lot that I may not be able to provide, and sometimes they even make assumptions about my personality due to my giftedness.**

—Boy, 14, Kentucky

My parents do not expect as much from me because I have had older siblings who were very intelligent, so they trust the fact that I will not make stupid mistakes and throw my life away. When other adults encounter the fact that I'm gifted, they drop most of the teenage stereotypes and ask me questions about what I like.

—Boy, 14, Ohio

**I have a strong suspicion that some adults are intimidated by gifted children. I have been belittled and had my opinions undervalued because of my age. I have utmost respect for adults who are wise enough to value my opinions and ideas without discrimination.**

—Girl, 14, Wisconsin

## YOUR TURN

When was the first time you noticed that you *were not* the smartest person in the room? Gifted students who are placed in classes with kids of varied levels of intellect are often shocked—*shocked!*—when they first encounter an environment where *everyone else* is as smart or smarter than they are. Reflect on the feelings you had when you first realized that there were some people your age whose intellectual capabilities rivaled or surpassed yours. Then, think of some advice you would give to a younger gifted person who was panicked at the thought of not being the all-knowing, perfect student—and deliver that advice to someone who needs to hear it (a younger gifted sibling, perhaps).

When I was little, like 3 or 4, people would tell me I would be the first scientist on Saturn or would invent a cure for cancer. That was really hard for me, because I thought I had to accomplish all these things they expected of me. Once my parents figured out how hard it was for me to hear these comments, they got people to stop saying things like that, which helped a lot.

—Boy, 15, North Carolina

**My mother expects sporadic bouts of genius followed by moments of incredible idiocy—which often happens. Outside of my gifted program teacher, my other teachers see me as a disappointment (at best) and at worst, they see me as a rebel who must be disciplined at all costs.**

**—Boy, 16, Iowa**

Teachers expect performance, responsibility, and an overall compliance to authority. Parents expect adult wisdom and responsibility, but with an occasional burst of childish behavior. Friends expect support and a general connectedness without bringing a lot of attention down on them for having a gifted friend (or being gifted themselves). Overall, it's pretty exhausting trying to fit all these protocols!

—Girl, 16, New York

**I got my first zero on a homework assignment that I had actually done, due to my not understanding my teacher's instructions. My mother hung this paper on the refrigerator and we all got a good laugh out of it.**

**—Girl, 19, Texas**

My mom always says, "If you're so smart, why do you act so dumb?" I know she's not calling me dumb, but nevertheless, this comment puts added pressure on me.

—Girl, 19, Pennsylvania

## YOUR TURN

Some things are just impossible, right? No matter how hard you try, they can't be done. Try disproving this by using your smartphone or a digital camera to take photographs of 10 things that *cannot* be photographed. For example, go outside and take a picture of:

- justice,
- prejudice,
- intelligence,
- time,
- honor,

- pity,
- infinity,
- transformation, and
- obsolescence.

Next, challenge yourself with some other impossibilities by photographing:

- 1,000,000 of something,
- communication between you and a nonliving object, or
- a place that doesn't exist.

Compile these photographs into a collage and ask some of your friends who have also done this activity with you to determine which photographs match the above descriptions. This activity should help you understand that reaching for the stars—and getting there—is not so futile after all.

We shift from the external perspective about giftedness (including expectations others have for you, a gifted person) to the inside view (what impact these outwardly experienced perceptions have on you, *the* gifted person).

As you read through the comments in this section, look for any trends in reactions to making mistakes based on age or gender. Does it appear that younger or older kids are harder on themselves when it comes to accepting their imperfections? Do boys or girls have a more realistic attitude toward the inevitability of making mistakes?

## How do others react when you make a mistake? How do you react?

Adults are disappointed when I make a mistake. I just wish they would cut me a little slack sometimes.
—Girl, 13, Maine

**My friends are often amused or, I think, relieved when I do poorly on a test or essay. I'd be happier getting average grades than good ones, because it would probably indicate that I am learning something at school.**

**—Girl, 14, Massachusetts**

My friends act like Armageddon has arrived when I mess up. But hey . . . I'm human, too.
—Boy, 14, Texas

**When I make a mistake, I'm probably harder on myself than anyone else is on me. My friends almost gloat about it when they see I've faltered, and that hurts.**

**—Girl, 16, New York**

My parents get pretty mad when I make a low B. (I guess they'll be unpleasantly surprised today—it's report card day.)
—Boy, 16, Tennessee

**Mistakes are a part of life. But, I try to make sure that means other people's lives. I make sure I am right before answering. I never just guess, even if that is what I tell people. I spend a lot of time learning things so I know. And I worry that I'll get caught someday not paying attention, and this will ruin my day.**

**—Boy, 13, Vermont**

I guess I always want to be better than last time, so if I make a stupid mistake I think, "Oh, this is really bad. I'm turning stupid. I am capable of so much more." For that reason, getting a B is very hard for me to accept.
—Girl, 14, Illinois

**When I make a mistake, my own reaction usually depends on how big it is. Usually, if I just get something wrong, I just feel embarrassed, but if someone else remarks upon it, it will ruin my entire day.**
**—Girl, 16, Wisconsin**

I used to get really frustrated and embarrassed. Other people seemed not to care, but I thought they did. Now, I just put another mark in my column of experience.
—Girl, 18, Virginia

**Nonacademic situations, like sports and music, have taught me that it's okay to make mistakes.**
**—Boy, 18, Utah**

It's okay to make mistakes. The important part is to learn why the mistake was made and how to fix it.
—Girl, 18, Beijing, China

# YOUR TURN

Think back on something in your life—playing a sport or musical instrument, learning a math concept or foreign language—that you struggled with at first. How did you react to this struggle? Did you give up and move on to something easier? Did you persevere and tackle the challenge despite the initial obstacles? Looking back on your reactions, would you do anything differently? Why or why not?

When I was younger, there were a lot of things I would refuse to do for fear of making a mistake and looking stupid in front of others. Even now, there are times when I won't speak out in class for fear of being wrong.

—Girl, 19, North Carolina

# YOUR TURN

Sometimes, people are more willing to take risks and accept failure in particular situations. For example, if you are self-assured about your intellect, you might be willing to take a hard class in high school, but if you think you're not as smart as everyone says you are, you might *not* be as willing to enroll in such a difficult course. The same is true in other arenas of life. For example, how willing are you to take:

- intellectual risks such as taking a hard class,
- physical risks such as trying out for a sports team for the first time,
- social risks such as sticking up for a classmate getting bullied, or
- emotional risks such as telling someone how you really feel about him or her?

Once you've considered your comfort level in each of the above categories of risk, ask yourself what you are gaining or losing by making the choices you have. This introspection may or may not change the way you make future decisions, but it may give you a better understanding of why you make the decisions you do.

# ACHIEVEMENT AND PERFECTIONISM

People who have studied gifted children and adults often identify personality characteristics that appear frequently among this population. Two of the more common characteristics mentioned are these:

★ *perfectionism*: the belief that *everything* you do has to be completed at the utmost level of performance. An A– if you can earn an A+?: Sorry . . . not good enough.

★ *supersensitivity*: the gifted person's vulnerability to criticism from others, as well as self-doubts about one's own level of competence, when it comes to feeling successful and "smart enough."

These personality characteristics often become the focus of many people's work on and assumptions about the gifted. We turn the tables a bit here by asking a question that is a little out of bounds (but fun to think about) when it comes to the stellar performance that others assume giftedness is all about.

## Can a person overachieve?

Those who overachieve are the ones who like to finish work about a week in advance. Their work must be the greatest and done to the fullest. An overachiever can sometimes take on too many things and still expect them all to be completed in a second—*everything* has to be their absolute best.

—Boy, 13, Texas

**One thing that annoys me is the kid who always has his hand up yelling, "OOOH! OOOH!" Now *that* kid is an over-achiever!**
**—Boy, 13, Minnesota**

**YOUR TURN**

In your own life, do perfectionism and/or supersensitivity come into play to any significant degree? If so, what impact do these traits have on your academic life and social interactions? If these characteristics don't describe you well, what *other* words would you use in describing your attitudes toward confronting challenges in school and in other situations?

No, a person cannot overachieve. I believe that if you set your goals high, you will go much further in life. Always remember that to get where you want to go you need a little bit of gas and a whole lot of knowledge. (That's my mom's philosophy. She's not a *real* philosopher, but I think she's a very smart woman.)

—Girl, 13, Ohio

**There are some kids in our gifted program who will start to cry or get mad if they get a 95% on a paper. These kids need to calm down and not worry so much. Not many good things come out of overachieving.**
**—Boy, 14, Kansas**

When someone tries extra hard on a simple assignment, that's overachievement. Also, when people write essays with big words instead of simple ones and creative ones, that's overachievement.

—Boy, 14, Iowa

**A person is overachieving when he or she is doing so much that it interferes with their life.**
**—Girl, 14, Pennsylvania**

Yes, a person can put too much pressure on herself and force herself to work harder. She may find out that the only person who appreciates this achievement level is herself—no one else.

—Girl, 14, Oklahoma

**I would call overachieving "putting forth all the effort you can"—just trying your best and maybe including a little bit of extra material. I'm not sure why people would call that "overachievement."**

**—Boy, Ohio, 14**

I suppose they can. They can stretch themselves too thin and run themselves ragged without all the pieces that they need to be complete.

—Girl, 15, Australia

**I do not believe a person can overachieve. You can achieve more than you had planned, but this is not overachievement. I think "overachievement" should be deleted from the English language and no longer be used in schools.**

**—Boy, 15, Pennsylvania**

As a gifted student and something of a perfectionist, I face pressure from myself and others to do better than I ever have before . . . to *always* do better. If I do badly on a homework assignment or a quiz, I wonder how this is possible if the class is so easy, and I think I must be turning stupid. For me, every improvement means almost nothing; it just supports what I already know. But every bad grade makes me think that I am becoming a failure. How else do I respond to this than to overachieve?

—Girl, 15, Illinois

**Yeah. If someone does so much that it gets too stressful for them, or if they do things just because grades are the only thing they really care for, not people or hobbies, that is overachieving.**

**—Boy, 15, Connecticut**

No one can overachieve. Overachievement is a term created by lazy people.

—Girl, 16, Ohio

**I understand the meaning of overachievement, but at the same time, how does that even make sense? To achieve is to perform or carry on with success, so if you are capable of doing that, how can that be too much accomplishment?**

**—Girl, 16, Alabama**

Yes, people overachieve when they spend so much time on work that they fail to remember that things other than their goals exist in life.

—Boy, 17, Tennessee

# TURNING THE TABLES . . . AGAIN

As the student comments in the above section show, there is no consensus on whether the concept of "overachievement" is a legitimate one. "To achieve more than one is capable of" seems to be a rather sticky definition of this multisyllabic word—especially when we ask gifted individuals for their input on the issue.

Let's briefly introduce a term that *is* commonly used by researchers and the general public alike as they disdainfully deal with gifted and talented individuals who for some reason do not fit the expectations others hold for them. The term is "underachievement," and the underachiever label is one worn by many gifted individuals who seem to dance to the beat of a different drummer.

There are several books on underachievement and underachievers that have been written describing tendencies and behaviors and offering potential solutions to the dilemma. You can Google the term and receive more than a million options to explore.

We asked a group of gifted teens about the term underachievement and what it meant to be an underachiever. Here are a few of their responses.

**Other people decide when to inflict the label of underachievement upon a person. I have been called an underachiever several times when I decided to put efforts into one subject or project and not another.**

**—Girl, 14, Ohio**

Teachers are well known for making this comment to try to coerce gifted kids into performing a task. Or, for not performing according to expectations. The label then travels like wildfire from class to class and you constantly have to battle the fallout through your school life. Why is it that other people get to decide your fate for you? Why can't you decide where, when, and how to use your energy to learn?

—Boy, 16, Michigan

**Some call it underachievement. I call it personal allocation of resources to areas of interest or passion. It hurts when a person (usually an adult) makes this judgment without even trying to understand the reason for less-than-stellar effort in an area. I choose where, when, and if I will put effort into something.**

**There are cases where I have invested fully only to realize that the area really didn't intrigue me as much as I thought. When tethering back and withdrawing my effort, the underachievement label was firmly planted by others. However, this was a better label to wear than failure, in my book!**
**—Girl, 17, Nevada**

Like the word gifted, no one really explains that underachieve is a derogatory and demeaning term. I think it is a two-punch combination made by people who already look down on you for the perception of having something they don't—giftedness—then are happy to point out when you lack effort, don't work to potential, or give up too easily on a task.
—Boy, 17, Illinois

Underachievement, like beauty, is in the eye of the beholder. We would like to leave you with one observation we have made through our work over the years. We have never met any gifted individual who rose in the morning (or afternoon—in the case of many teens who can get away with it) and set out to underachieve in life.

# GIFTED KIDS GROWN UP

Every year since 1964, one rising high school senior boy and girl from each state have been selected as Presidential Scholars—more than 14,000 students in total. Each candidate is selected due to high academic performance and off-the-charts test scores. A researcher named Dr. Felice Kaufmann decided to follow up on some of these scholars—the group selected between 1964–1968—and find out how they are doing 40 years after having been identified as an outstanding student back in high school.

Dr. Kaufmann located 427 of these scholars, and 145 chose to participate in her 1980 follow-up survey. Here are some of the findings:

★ 33% lived in rural areas or towns with populations under 50,000;

★ 21% lived in cities of more than 1 million people;

★ 81% were married or in a marriage-like relationship;

★ 23% had no children;

★ 73% had earned advanced degrees, either a doctorate or its equivalent;

★ the participants' chosen occupations varied greatly, from the typically-expected doctors, lawyers, and educators, to others who chose diverse careers such as stock brokers, office managers, farmers, writers, artists, musicians, philosophers, homemakers, politicians (a state governor and an international ambassador), and therapists;

★ 80% reported having derived great enjoyment from their work. Only one individual reported getting little enjoyment from working;

★ 59% reported having had some difficulties as adults with academic, social, or personal problems related to their abilities or achievement; and

★ 33% said that, all things considered, they were very satisfied in life; 53% described themselves as satisfied, and 13% as not satisfied.

Gifted individuals run the gamut in life. We hope that by reading about Dr. Kaufmann's work here, you realize that growing up gifted has some unique twists and turns, but also many qualities shared by anyone gaining more responsibilities and independence. There are challenges each of us face that become defining moments or interesting footnotes in our lives. We leave this section with a few examples of contemporary gifted (and talented) individuals who have met life's challenges and endured.

# LADY GAGA GAGGED

Of all of Lady Gaga's accomplishments, her most enduring one might be this: perseverance. Here's why: L. A. Reid, former president of Def Jam Records, reports that he stalled Lady Gaga's musical pursuits early in her career. After signing her to a record contract, Reid released her from it several months later after hearing her demo songs: "It was a work in progress and I was having a bad day. I said, 'You know, I really don't like (her music). You know, let her have her freedom. Let her have her career" (Johnson, 2011, para. 5).

Lady Gaga cried for an entire day after hearing the news, but she moved on, ultimately signing a record deal with Interscope Records, a company that supported her artistically and helped her end up one of pop music's biggest stars.

Lady Gaga is not the only artist to receive early rejection. So did the following:

➤ *Alicia Keys*, whose contract with Columbia Records was terminated after 2 years. She eventually moved on to Arista Records.

➤ *50 Cent*, whose recording contract was canceled after he was shot nine times. The rapper stated, "I had just signed with Columbia Records and they dropped me because of the shooting. I could deal with every bullet wound but I (couldn't) take that" (Johnson, 2011, para. 14). Within 2 years, 50 Cent teamed with Dr. Dre and Eminem, making him one of rap's most successful artists.

➤ *Beyoncé*, who began her career with Destiny's Child, joined Elektra Records, but was dropped by them shortly thereafter, causing Beyoncé to work even harder. When Destiny's Child made their debut in the Will Smith movie *Men in Black*, they were soon signed by Columbia Records, going on to set sales records for girl groups and spawning Beyoncé's solo career, including several multiplatinum albums (Johnson, 2011).

# TABULA RASA

Tabula Rasa is a Latin term translated into English as "blank slate." In essence, it refers to the way that something (or someone) is before it is influenced and changed by outside forces like family, friends, school, and the world in general.

Another way to think of tabula rasa is to finish some statements by writing down your first thoughts that come to mind upon reading them. Recently, a group of 30+ gifted high school sophomores and juniors did just this in completing the following statements. As you read these responses, consider how you might respond to this blank slate of intriguing ideas.

If I could change one thing about my life . . .

★ it would to be more open-minded and accepting.

★ I'd want my parents to have the lives they wanted.

★ I would spend less time in school.

★ I wouldn't be sad anymore.

★ I would be taller!

If I could change one thing about our world . . .

★ I would live in a busy, opportunity-filled city.

★ I would change human nature so that it wasn't so violent.

★ I would put less emphasis on schooling and more on thinking and learning

★ I would make society more accepting of gifted people.

★ I would want more worldwide stability.

When I get an A in school . . .

★ I don't care.

★ no one cares—I always get A's.

★ it's normal for me, so I don't get overly excited.

When I hear the word "gifted," I think . . .

★ me!

★ strange.

★ that I wasn't "gifted" until seventh grade!

If I could convince my teachers of one thing . . .

★ stop telling me to work harder.

★ it would be that yelling doesn't help.

★ I would get them to know that busy work is pointless.

I do best in school when . . .

★ I have intelligent teachers.

★ I enjoy the subject.

★ I'm with other smart people (including the teacher).

My social life . . .

★ is nonexistent.

★ is complicated and atypical.

★ is busy, saucy, and fun.

★ is none of your concern.

Most of my friends expect me . . .

★ to listen.

★ to be good at everything.

★ to be me.

When I consider my future . . .

★ I think about being a teacher.

★ I think medical field!

★ I feel emotionally and intrapersonally unprepared.

★ I consider everything.

★ I have no idea what I am going to do.

The worst part about being gifted . . .

★ being bored in school.

★ people try to take advantage of me.

★ discrimination.

★ being gifted.

★ the expectations and assumptions.

★ sometimes I need more deep conversations instead of shallow ones.

The best part about being gifted . . .

★ I can do well in school without really trying.

★ being gifted.

★ people think you are smart.

★ I have no idea.

# SUMMARY

Key to this chapter was a focus on helping you recognize that internal expectations—yours—are much more important than external expectations—those things *other people* think you should do. In the high-brow world of educational research, the construct of motivation would now come into focus. We could cite results from study after study that state (with empirical significance, no less!) that high levels of motivation lead to successful endeavors and outcomes.

Well, duh! It doesn't take a long-term research project to realize that if a person is interested and engaged in exciting activities, he is not only likely to have some pretty positive outcomes, but he might also *enjoy* the process.

And potential? This word will be a recurring theme throughout this book. Don't be so focused on trying to reach something that will always be a moving target imposed by others. Develop your own drive. Find your interests and passions. Dream big and start making some of those dreams come to life. Remember, there are many people ready, willing, and able to dash your dreams in life. That is, *if you let them*!

Lastly, in case you were wondering how in the world we were able to make a disparate connection in a book about being gifted with Lady Gaga . . . she's gifted too! Stefani Germanotta (a.k.a. Lady Gaga) attended the Center for Talented Youth (CTY) program at Johns Hopkins University before becoming a pop superstar (Landau, 2010). Go figure!

# chapter 4

# THE MANY STORIES OF SCHOOL

It is important that students bring a certain ragamuffin, barefoot irreverence to their studies; they are not here to worship what is known, but to question it.

—J. Bronowski, *The Ascent of Man*

**IF** we say the word "school," what comes to mind? Some of you who have had mostly positive experiences with teachers will see school as a place where lots of learning occurs. Sure, there may be some necessary evils to endure (remember those timed multiplication/division tests?), yet your overall reaction to school leaves you smiling, not frowning. Others among you will see school as some sort of twisted prison where all manner of pointless tasks are required to be completed before that high school diploma is awarded. If this is the case, you'll see school as an endurance test rather than a creative challenge to be cherished. And for still other readers, school may not even be an actual building; with homeschooling and virtual schools increasing in popularity every year, your school may be as close as the den in your home where you take online tests to earn AP credits.

Whatever your reactions to the word "school," there is little doubt that your education has had its share of highlights and horror stories. In this chapter, we'll highlight both, using the words of gifted students to explain when education worked in their favor and when it did not.

However, our approach is not just to report on what happens—good or bad—in school. We hope to inspire you to take charge of your education and to take responsibility and ownership for your intellectual growth and progress. There's no need to feel victimized by educational situations that don't meet your learning or personal needs, but if you do nothing positive to address your dissatisfaction, it's likely that little will change for the better.

## Describe a typical school day . . .

In a typical school day, I'm usually rushing to get to my next class. Once I'm there, if I'm not learning something new, it can get pretty boring (but, my classes are usually fun). I usually get plenty of time to socialize between classes. At day's end, I just load up my backpack with homework and head for the bus.
—Girl, 13, Iowa

**On a typical school day, I learn many different things just so that I can get tested on them later to see if I was paying attention.**
**—Boy, 13, Nevada**

A typical day has me going to the gifted class and then two other classes before chorus. In chorus, I get picked on because I am smart and a little overweight. Then, lunch, recess, some more teasing, and the last three classes of the day. Finally, I ride the bus home with everyone screaming their heads off.

—Girl, 13, Ohio

**On a typical day, I just go to classes and do my work. Sometimes I have interesting conversations with people I don't know.**

**—Boy, 14, Texas**

Thirty-five minutes of boredom, six minutes of mild interests, and the rest of the period doing anything I can without: (a) getting into trouble, (b) the teacher noticing me, or (c) aggravating anyone around me. When I get a subject of mild interest to me, listen, and do the work, [it's] getting patted on the head for my seemingly effortless results. In sum, a typical day involves pain, a bit of isolation, and a lot of misery.

—Girl, 14, Australia

**I roll out of bed. Roll onto the bus. Bounce around the building like a pinball from class to class. Collect points as I go, and try to avoid trouble. In a typical day I can't recall learning anything at all.**

**—Boy, 14, Alabama**

First period: Spanish, which is usually fun, as we sing songs and present skits. English is also fun. In science, the teacher has the most helpless look, as the gifted students write and draw diagrams on the board to better explain or expand upon what the teacher just said. The teacher simply says, "This isn't AP, you know." In social studies, the entire class debates the decisions of the Aztecs. In math, I zone out and mess around with the equations while everyone else is still stuck on the basics.

—Girl, 14, New Jersey

**Typically, I walk into class and an assignment is on the board. The teacher tells you to do it and then gives you your homework. I then just wait for the next class in hopes of getting my day over with soon.**

**—Boy, 15, Colorado**

Lecture. Worksheet. Read from book and answer questions at end of chapter. Lecture with worksheet. Quiz on reading. Repeat.

—Girl, 16, Illinois

**A typical school day is boring and tedious, filled with repetitive work that it seems like we've been studying for years. It involves being forced to work with "partners" where you inevitably have to drag the other person along with you and then share your grade with them. My typical day is filled with frustration with other people's learning pace.**

**—Boy, 16, Iowa**

I go to boring classes that I don't feel are necessary. I get looked down on for raising my hand or knowing answers, so I simply sit there. Then we do group activities where I am stuck with all the work.

—Girl, 16, North Carolina

**My typical school day provides a certain comfort in repetitive motion and activity. I can be on autopilot and not worry about missing anything relevant. I can focus on the hall talk and feel no anxiety about schoolwork.**

**—Boy, 16, Maryland**

## YOUR TURN

### Chime in on Cheating

"A typical day in school involves a whole lot of cheating. It is rampant at my private college prep school," says 14-year-old Vincent. "I wonder what can be done to stop the cheating before temptation and the need to be competitive overcomes my sense of right and wrong?"

Is cheating to either get ahead or stay ahead a major issue in school? What do you think can be done to diminish cheating and/or avoid the temptation to cheat?

No highs, no lows, no drama. My typical day is business as usual, looking forward to the weekend. I wonder if this is all there is to life since my parents seem to follow the same pattern with their work?

—Girl, 17, Missouri

**Fill in the blanks. Write the letter of the correct answer. Complete the crossword puzzle. Ugh!**
**—Boy, 17, Wisconsin**

Typical is the monotonous, yet melodic babbling of knowledge as it flows from textbook to worksheet to student and back on the test.

—Boy, 17, California

And a perfect school day . . .

My perfect day would be when our GT program gets recognized for all the good it does for us instead of being cut because we are already ahead of the curve.

—Girl, 13, Ohio

**A perfect day would occur when I don't have to be the one to get *the* highest grade on a test or when someone gives a better answer than I can.**
**—Boy, 13, Nevada**

A perfect school day is when I get to move between as many or as few subjects as I would like to explore, and I get to do challenging work that is not simply handed to me on a platter.

—Girl, 13, Australia

**During a perfect school day, I would be treated like everyone else.**
**—Boy, 14, Washington**

Perfect? When our teachers would be Nobel Prize winners who ask us interesting questions, then let us try to figure out answers while they encourage discussion and thinking. The afternoon would be when we test our answers followed by a banquet where kids are awarded prizes for our daily brilliance, or at least for trying and making a bunch of mistakes but not giving up.
—Boy, 14, Utah

**A perfect school day would go by quickly and involve no homework, leaving me time for a long bath until I fall asleep reading.**
**—Girl, 15, Iowa**

A team of experts helps me design an experiment or project that I get to work on as long as I want—without being graded! And, I have an assistant to take notes for me as I work. That's the perfect day.
—Boy, 15, Vermont

**When we do group activities and actually learn something new as we bounce ideas off of one another. That's the perfect school day.**
**—Girl, 15, Ohio**

Perfect isn't school at all. It is nothing but fun and exploring whatever tickles your fancy.
—Boy, 15, Michigan

**Perfect is a place where I get to learn about my interests and can fly with my ideas instead of doing extra math because I'm not so good at it.**
**—Girl, 16, Hawaii**

In a perfect school day, the teachers would ask you what you want to learn and then provide the resources for you to do just that. Then, you would discuss your work directly with the teacher. Also, you could spend as much time on a topic as you want to.
—Boy, 16, Pennsylvania

Get there on time, not get embarrassed in any way, open my locker with ease, and have Mr. Mac as my sub in chemistry (he's the *best* sub!).
—Girl, 16, Pennsylvania

Perfect: Write an essay on what you feel about a topic important to you, look under the microscope and draw a picture of the organism, and read to your heart's content.
—Boy, 17, Wisconsin

I can go slow if I want, fast if I'm so inclined, or skip right to the end and work backwards sometimes too. A perfect day is where I am free to think flexibly and act at my own pace. Can you even do this in school?
—Girl, 17, Massachusetts

## YOUR TURN

What makes a perfect school day? Is it making school into something it is not? Or, is it not going to school at all? Jot down some characteristics a perfect school day might have. Then brainstorm three to five ways you can make your *typical* school day more like a perfect one.

What would it take to put just *two* of your brainstormed ideas into practice? Who would you need to involve/convince? What "rules" would need to be broken or changed? What impact *might* your changes have on the other students? The teachers? The administrators? The community?

Descriptions of a typical and a perfect school day are just that—descriptions. In the section that follows, we broaden the focus a bit to learn about challenges that gifted learners face in school. A striking realization is that many of the challenges involve things other than the curriculum.

## What are the biggest challenges in school for gifted learners?

We are more pressured to always do well in school and to set a good example for the other students—that's the biggest challenge.

—Boy, 13, Kansas

**Dealing with teachers who run away from extremely bright children is my greatest school challenge. Teachers should embrace students like these rather than try to form them into a seventh-grade stereotype. The next biggest challenge is to find students who can really be friends with me. Most kids my age are into how tight their jeans are, not the human response to the unknown.**

**—Boy, 13, New York**

I'm a year younger than my grade, and I'm in advanced classes, so when sophomores and juniors see me in their classes, they aren't always as polite as they could be. They say things like, "Wow! You must really be smart!" How do you respond to that? It's impossible.

—Girl, 13, Oklahoma

**My biggest challenge is moving between grades for my classes. Sometimes (often) I wish I was just a regular eighth grader and didn't need 11th-grade language arts at the high school. It's a pain to have to miss 10 minutes of class coming and going just to be with kids who are all 2 feet taller than me and look (and smell) like Neanderthals.**

**—Boy, 13, Wisconsin**

The most challenging aspect during school is trying not to impress somebody by doing their work or other things to show them that you are cool. Being a gifted student can put a lot of pressure on you to fit in.

—Girl, 14, Louisiana

One of the biggest challenges is that programs and services for gifted kids are being eliminated. In my district, the fourth- and fifth-grade program was cut this year due to money issues—the teacher was laid off. Are they going to send the kids somewhere else? Or are *we* just going to get nothing? The short answer is nothing.

—Boy, 14, Ohio

Organization and time management are my biggest challenges.

—Girl, 14, New Jersey

The biggest challenge is always having to do better. Say you get a really good grade on a report card. Now you are expected to do just as well or better the next 6 weeks. The 6 weeks get tougher and tougher but you are still expected to keep up your grades. No one really understands this except the students. "Gifted" might mean we're smart, but we still mess up and need breathing room.

—Boy, 14, Texas

The biggest challenge is finding the time to volunteer at causes I know are worthwhile. If you are gifted and believe you can use your gifts to better your community, by all means, get started! It's just finding the time that's so hard.

—Girl, 14, Washington

Making friends is tough. Kids are sometimes jealous and like to make fun of smart kids to cover their jealousy. It hurts sometimes.

—Boy, 14, Oregon

My biggest challenge is to not become lazy. I see a lot of my friends who used to make really good grades but now are flunking because they won't do work that is boring to them.

—Girl, 15, Colorado

**A tremendous challenge is curriculum that only focuses on passing state competency exams. Teaching to the test functionally shuts down advanced abilities.**
**—Boy, 15, Alabama**

Right now, I need time to follow my passions of religion and psychology. I want to read novels by Jane Austen, Tolstoy, and Dostoyevsky. I want to write a book for other gifted teenagers on ways we can improve our educational system. I just need time.
—Girl, 15, Illinois

**The biggest challenge is my complete lack of mental growth as I sit through the monotonous repetition of information I knew 3 or more years ago.**
**—Boy, 16, Missouri**

I've been homeschooled since kindergarten. In preschool, I was more interested in daydreaming, pretending, and doing my own thing. I was also the only kid there capable of writing my name, complete with nickname (Buttercup) and middle name. All my teachers and every other adult I came into contact with thought there was something wrong with me and that my mom had to do something to "fix" me, because I'd be very unhappy in my school career if I didn't change. Well, my mom and I liked me the way I was, thank you very much, and so we decided to homeschool.

Of course, it helped my learning. I was able to read many adult-level books on whatever topics I was interested in (mainly science), as well as having more time to spend on violin, writing, dancing, and, surprisingly enough, with friends! But the most important part of homeschooling was that I didn't have to feel I had to change myself in order to be accepted by others. I didn't have to face criticism for all the things that were a fundamental part of my personality, and so until fifth grade (when I went to a private school for 3 years), I was able to be emotionally healthy.

I don't think homeschoolers need to be brought back into the system. The fact that they are opting out will cause the public schools to make adjustments or lose students (and money). The reasons I opted out are that in school there is little room for creativity, original thinking, or independent learning. In high school (I spent a year there), I learned almost nothing but was forced to spend hours doing homework on the order of worksheets. I think there should be fewer worksheets and lectures taken directly out of the textbook and more discussion and independent reading, like is done in college.

—Girl, 16, Illinois

**Plain and simple—social interactions and raging teen hormones.**

**—Girl, 16, North Dakota**

The total disconnect between what people think I should know and what I am capable of learning. I want to soar, not wallow in a trough of indifference.

—Girl, 17, Virginia

**The biggest challenge is trying to stay focused on the present because we are always thinking of our futures. Losing sight of my childhood is a concern.**

**—Boy, 17, Georgia**

Putting up with 12 years of education that we could learn in 4 years.

—Boy, 18, California

# A LITTLE TOO MUCH KNOWLEDGE AND UNDERSTANDING?

Cleo, a gifted teen we know, shared the following experience during a social studies test covering the Civil War:

Based on our readings and your experience, which one of the following is the main reason for the Civil War in the United States?

(a) Slavery

(b) Class differences between the North and South

(c) Economic inequality

(d) The change from agriculture to industry

Said Cleo, "Here's how I thought about which answer was best:

"Okay, I remember the book saying that slavery was the main reason, but in yesterday's review our teacher did talk about Southerners' feelings that the North was trying to destroy the way of life in the South. To me, this means 'b' is also correct.

"And, last night while I was watching Ken Burns's show about the Civil War on PBS, discussion centered on the big picture of the agrarian economy of the South versus the industrial ways of life in the North. And, in our ASPIRE (GT) class, we've all been talking about how the economy can only grow if people begin buying things made here in our country. Since the South was pretty self-sufficient with their plantations but cotton crop prices were falling, maybe it really *was* economic inequality that caused the Civil War.

"All the answers are right! But which is the best answer?

"I ended up choosing 'b' because it seemed to be the most general idea that all the other answers could fall under as categories. I got the question wrong. The answer was 'a.' I explained my answer to the teacher, but she said my thinking was way off base and every-one knew slavery was the main reason. I never argued about an answer I got wrong on a test in any class for the rest of the year. I felt so dumb for not knowing the obvious."

## YOUR TURN

Is Cleo's experience one that you have shared? Has this experience changed the way you do things in your life? What would you say to Cleo if you wanted to provide some advice?

# CREATIVITY AND BOREDOM

One of the terms that heads this section—"boredom"—is the bane of every gifted learner facing the experience of a mind-numbing curriculum. The other term, "creativity," offers hope that something good lies beneath the surface of learning. Read on to learn how by inserting creativity into their educational equations, these students saw education as being something more than amassing a collection of unrelated facts.

**Does being creative ever get in the way of learning in school? Does it ever get you in trouble?**

If you are not creative, you end up earning better grades. Being creative means making things harder than they have to be.

—Girl, 13, Kansas

**Depending on the individual teacher and information, being creative can work for or against you. Last year, I had the most amazing English teacher. She would just let us write, every day. Everyone in the class had their creative horizons expanded massively. It was then that I first learned the joy of speaking to someone's soul through a form of art. This year has been plagued by standardized testing (*please* don't get me started!) and when I took the extra time to incorporate rhythmic motif into my poem, my English teacher scolded me, saying I should not use rhythmic motif if we have not covered it in class. That hurt me.**

**—Boy, 13, New York**

In elementary school, I could never pass a timed test in math, because I was always looking for patterns instead of just solving problems.

—Girl, 14, New Jersey

**Yes and no. If you have a tendency to doodle and not listen when you're drawing, you can get in trouble. But, if you are in art class and you are doodling in a good way, you'll get a high grade.**

**—Boy, 14, Arizona**

Creativity only gives me trouble in math. You have to do the problems in a certain way, and when I get the right answer by using another method, I get marked wrong.

—Girl, 14, Ohio

In a sense, being creative gets in the way in that creative people are forced to choose between creating meaningful things and doing schoolwork. I live to write, but I am forced to choose between doing my homework and writing, because I have no time to do both. Often, school makes me so tired that when I get home, I have no energy left to create.

—Boy, 14, Illinois

Being creative enhances my learning. I stay with ideas and information, exploring in depth. This helps me not only process but also adapt information to make it my own. In school, this approach is anathema. I am expected to recall facts and figures, but not to think because this approach might deviate from expected test answers.

—Girl, 14, Nevada

I am not artistically creative, but I am verbally and socially creative. For example, if I've known you for a little while, I can pick you out the perfect birthday present or mix you an awesome CD. Or, if you give me a topic I can write a mean essay. And yes, this can get me in trouble at school. I've frequently been criticized for my creativity, most specifically in writing. I have learned to find out the style of each teacher and conform my style to suit what [he or she wants] in order to earn an A.

—Girl, 15, Indiana

Multiple choice tests don't allow for any creativity. Sometimes I just make up my own answer and circle it, because none of the other answers are really good ones. My teachers don't like this.

—Boy, 15, Colorado

Learning schoolwork is overrated. It is more like review of every year over and over—like in the movie *Groundhog Day*! Being creative allows me to look like I'm content at school, while deviously involved in my

own mental gymnastics. For example, I am working on how the flight patterns of flocks of birds follow properties of fluid mechanics. This happens in my head while my body moves from one subject to another in the assembly line of high school.
—**Girl, 15, Virginia**

School is what I do. Creative is who I am.
—Boy, 15, North Carolina

**My creativity is my release from the mundane; my ability to avoid the lobotomizing effects of teaching to the test; my means of knowing I am here, in this world. Does it get me in trouble? It just did. I am headed to the office yet again for not paying attention and writing instead of doing math.**
—**Boy, 16, Florida**

I used to be really creative when writing stories in English, but as I got older, things changed. I was no longer graded on my creativity, but on how much the teacher liked my writing. And usually, when a teacher was boring, they didn't like to read things that dealt with fairies or anything else nonhuman.
—Girl, 16, Georgia

**I've often been caught daydreaming in history class about what it would've been like to live in Roman times. I have a tendency to take the helm and plow**

---

# YOUR TURN

Creativity can be described in many different ways. How do you define creativity? Using your definition, are you creative? How might others answer this question about you?

There are also many ways to be creative—music, art, writing, storytelling, inventing, acting, composing, choreography, and any number of other options. How would others describe your way(s) to be creative? How can you describe ways your friends or family members are creative?

ahead, charting my own course from A to B, and possibly detouring at D or Z in order to get to B another way. Many people have problems with this.

—Boy, 16, Minnesota

I believe everyone is creative in [his or her] own ways, and my way is dance. I want to pursue dance after high school, but no one whatsoever has helped me. In the eyes of my parents and teachers, I'm a dumb little girl who wants to jump around for a living and isn't serious because she's so caught up in her little dream.

—Girl, 16, California

**Creativity adds spice to my days. I sprinkle my work with the imaginations of my mind, which enhances everything I do. In English and social studies, this is fine. In math, there isn't much room to wiggle around solving problems. In science, my mind wanders to exploring ideas. This causes some problems for me since I want to try two or three alternatives to an experimental process, but my teacher just wants the lab report done according to the written procedure. Funny, I can't see how anything can be discovered following so many rules.**

**—Girl, 16, Idaho**

Sometimes, being creative means you have opinions that can get out of hand, as they are not considered socially or politically correct. Happens to me.

—Boy, 17, Tennessee

**Oh yes, creativity can get in the way in school! A lot of times teachers expect one certain answer that they consider the "right" answer. When a gifted individual comes up with a creative answer or solution to a problem, teachers may not take the time to hear you out because they are tied to believing only their own answer.**

**—Girl, 17, Maryland**

**Are you ever bored in school? If so, what do you do to relieve the boredom?**

Incessantly. I tend to do two or three other tasks at my desk to keep myself mentally moving. The game is on when the teachers call on me to try to catch me off task. I have a pretty good track record of winning these battles.

—Girl, 13, Georgia

I think that school does not understand my passion for knowledge. For example, we will go over Shay's Rebellion but we won't discuss how the rebellion set a precedent for citizen political expression. We will discuss Sir Isaac Newton, but we will not examine how he influenced not only science in Europe, but also music, art, architecture, and even literature. I am worried that I will never be stimulated academically until college. (I am sure this is not an uncommon lament). My older sister says "it will get harder in high school," but I am skeptical. When she says "harder" she means "more work," not necessarily more stimulating work.

—Boy, 14, New York

A better question to ask is, "Are there ever times when you are *not* bored in school?" The answer? Yes, during music.

—Girl, 14, Ontario

I got bored once in sixth grade. My teacher was explaining some math, and I fell asleep while he was talking because I already knew what he was talking about. He yelled at me and ordered me to wake up. I did the work and got 100 percent. He got even madder at me that I wasn't paying attention, but still got a good grade.

—Boy, 14, Utah

I used to be a great student who always did his work, but after a while school got so boring that I just started acting up. School did not (does not) matter to me anymore.

—Boy, 14, Texas

**It's always "been there, done that." It hasn't been so bad this particular semester, but in the first half of the year I quite literally thought I was going to die of apathy and sluggishness brought on by lack of mental exercise. The only way I survived was through constant writing and constantly setting new challenges for myself.**

**—Girl, 14, Australia**

Why do teachers assume at the beginning of the year that we have lost all knowledge from previous years?

—Boy, 14, New Jersey

**I get bored when I am sitting near the back of the room. It makes it difficult to keep my mind on the subject when I am so far away from it.**

**—Boy, 15, Ohio**

I can see through teachers' attempts to just make us busy or fulfill state requirements or try to make us do better on standardized tests.

—Girl, 15, Minnesota

**In one class, the teacher repeats the same information in answer to questions from classmates who don't bother to listen the first time. I think he should arrange to repeat himself after class, not during.**

**—Boy, 15, North Carolina**

I often find myself bored in school, mainly in American History. To relieve the boredom, I either stare into the blank faces of my classmates or act out inappropriately. I don't believe this is what I should be doing, but my boredom often gets the best of me.

—Boy, 16, Iowa

**I tank up on extracurricular options. Being heavily involved in social activities reduces the percentage of my day associated with coursework, which is the same as boredom. The percentage of boredom is down to like 40% instead of the 100% (well, 90% if I count lunch in there) that existed when I wasn't extra-curricularly challenged.**

—**Girl, 16, Pennsylvania**

School becomes boring when a teacher is explaining something trivial to someone who was just too lazy to take notes or read the material. I used to read in class when I got bored, but no more—that offends teachers.

—Boy, 17, Nebraska

**Bored is a lack of focus on anything but knowledge-level knowing. I find it uncanny that students never complain of boredom when socializing or doing things focused on belonging, discussing issues, or involving their emotional judgments. I even see bored teachers. So, why do we endure this systemic issue? Oh yes—proficiency tests!**

—**Girl, 17, Virginia**

B is for banality—ignorance and bliss.
O is for original—a "take" I hope exists.
R is for redundancy—my life from day to day.
E is for extraneous—to strive for more than this.
D is for delivery—still waiting in hope I pray.
A cute little *ditty* I hope you can share with others. BORED is a state of mind and experience we students should not have to endure because "you will need to know this in the future."

—Boy, 17, California

Life seldom gives you challenges sequentially. More often than not, you get bombarded with situations that demand your attention simultaneously—whether or not you are ready to face them. Jamie's story is one example of how a gifted young woman with multiple learning needs confronted her education in the midst of *other* life changes affecting her family. "Jamie's Juggling Act," you might call it. In the end, it is Jamie's perseverance and the help she received from competent, caring adults that led her down some interesting, worthwhile life paths.

# Jamie McKinseley
## Considering Homeschooling

I went to public school through third grade, but I had issues. I was always above grade level in reading and always behind in math. I had difficulty staying on task in class, but it wasn't that I was distracted. There was so much going on that I had a hard time keeping up with it all.

I would get behind on my classwork, which meant most of my recesses were spent inside catching up on math instead of running around with other kids. I felt I was being punished because I couldn't do what was expected at the same speed and in the same way everyone else was doing it. Memorize addition, subtraction, multiplication, and division tables? Why?

I was continually chided for not working to my potential—whatever that meant! After third grade, my moms and I decided to homeschool.

Yes, I did say "moms"—I have two of them.

To me, family is an unconventional mix of people. I have what is called an open adoption. This means I have frequent contact with my birth mother while I live with my adoptive mother.

When I was young, this was a little confusing, but my birth mom and I didn't have a lot of contact then. It did become a big deal to me, though, when my adoptive parents divorced when I was 4 years old—I thought it was my fault.

At that point, both of my moms thought it would be a good idea to get involved to help me over the trauma. I eventually understood that my life was very special and that having two moms helped me become very unique.

Most of you don't have multiple moms to deal with in your lives, but your family might be considering homeschooling. This is a big decision that will impact your life, so don't take it casually. Talk to your parents. Get involved in the decision. And get online and explore what sorts of things are done by homeschoolers. Here are some key questions we considered when exploring the homeschooling option:

> ➤ *Why are we doing this*? Is it parent issues with the school curriculum, religious beliefs, or student nonacademic issues like bullying? Kids need to have input and know what is going on.

> *What is the learning plan?* What local and state requirements have to be met? A detailed written plan is critical—for both you and your homeschooling parents.

> *Can you join extracurriculars (i.e., clubs, sports, the arts) in the school district where you would be enrolled if you weren't homeschooling?* What opportunities exist for you to get involved?

> *Is there a local homeschooling group? What do they do?* Some get families together for educational experiences, field trips, or to socialize. It's important not to be isolated.

Key to my homeschooling commitment was the ability to add my two cents about it, as my moms included me in all of the discussions and decisions about homeschooling. We worked through possible arrangements and solutions to some difficulties we might face, like whether to follow an integrated curriculum or focus on each content area separately. (We decided on more integration since I had a few years of bad experience in a separate content setting.)

As time went on, my educational plan incorporated volunteer work. At the age of 11, I was volunteering in a neurofeedback clinic with underprivileged kids from troubled families where we used finger painting as therapy to channel their emotions onto the page. One of my moms worked there as a research nurse and wanted me to realize I had a lot going for me in life, and I should give back to others less fortunate. It was love at first try.

I have continued volunteering in the clinic, and now I am in charge of the art therapy component of the program. We put on art shows at the clinic and in local galleries, where the kids' work is featured and, in some cases, sold. It is very fulfilling to see how a sense of family develops between the volunteers and the kids in the program. And the joy on the kids' faces when people fawn over their artwork is amazing.

I rematriculated to public high school when I was 15. It was a transition, but I did keep contact with lots of friends from my homeschooling days, so it wasn't like I was dropped in from some other planet. And I had both of my moms helping me with my new schooling situation.

If you believe in your dreams and follow your heart, you can accomplish anything you want. You just have to trust in yourself and communicate clearly about your needs. This is where homeschooling really worked for me. I was able to get involved beyond reading and studying, which made my learning real, and I learned how to be a strong advocate for my needs.

*Jamie McKinseley is a 16-year-old honors student in a Northeastern public school who thrived as a homeschooler. Jamie plans on attending college to be a social worker, clinical psychologist, or perhaps international banker (following in her other mom's footsteps to become a philanthropist).*

# TENDENCIES OF TEACHERS

Bob (one of your authors) has been accused of being "elitist" or "confrontational" when correcting instructors who claim to be "gifted teachers." He often points out that the correct reference should be "teachers of the gifted," and that there is a difference.

In this section, you get to experience how gifted students describe the individuals charged with providing guidance on their journey toward learning.

## What makes a "gifted teacher"?

A gifted teacher is someone who enjoys teaching, who can get kids under control easily while still having fun, and who has ways to make the classroom "come alive" by [his or her] enthusiasm and knowledge.
—Girl, 13, Maine

**A gifted teacher can get you interested in anything, even if it's only a brick.**
—**Boy, 13, Iowa**

Gifted teachers are those who aren't intimidated by kids who are smarter than they are.
—Girl, 13, Texas

**They understand how stressed students can get at times because they have been there themselves.**
—**Boy, 13, Maine**

I think a gifted teacher should be able to relate to gifted children either by being gifted themselves or having their own gifted children. You don't know gifted until you live it (or with it).

—Girl, 14, Ohio

**If they have the ability to tie things in and make them fun, while allowing leniency for random discussions that add to the class, and if they are able to get any student hooked on a subject, whatever it is, then they are gifted.**

**—Boy, 14, Connecticut**

Gifted teachers aren't necessarily gifted in the same way a student might be. Their giftedness tends to be based more upon their style, as they are able to do these things: relate the subject matter to the students' lives, devise interesting areas for exploration, and create an atmosphere in the classroom where the students really want to be there. No subject, no matter how tempting to the student, remains interesting with a dull teacher.

—Girl, 14, Australia

# YOUR TURN

Steve Jobs, founder of Apple Inc., spoke about how his fourth-grade teacher changed his life. In an article in *Rolling Stone* published shortly after his death, he is quoted as saying, "Ms. Hill was one of the saints of my life. She taught an advanced class and it took her about a month to get hip to my situation. She bribed me into learning" (Broome, 2011, p. 1). She did bribe him (literally!) with candy and $5 bills from her own money. He quickly became hooked on learning, skipped fifth grade, and went straight to middle school.

When you think back on your own education, do you have a Ms. Hill in your past? A teacher who went further than he or she had to go to engage you in learning? If so, write a letter to this person—a real letter—and locate someone who knows how to contact this individual. Then, send or deliver this letter of thanks to the Ms. Hill in your life. Trust us, it will matter.

**I don't know. I've never had one.**

—Girl, 14, Ontario

I have had some really gifted teachers who can deal with difficult situations without losing their tempers or sending kids to the office. Those are gifted teachers to me.

—Boy, 15, Minnesota

**There are many people who can be teachers, but only certain people in the world are gifted at teaching. These few just seem able to express themselves and what they are trying to teach more easily. I think of these teachers as the ones that you remember when you get older. Not only do they teach you school lessons, they teach you life lessons.**

—Girl, 15, Oklahoma

When I was 10 years old, I took AP calculus BC. On the first exam, I answered all 10 questions in about 10 minutes. When I turned in my test with the 10 answers (which were all correct), Mr. F asked me, "Where's your work?" I asked, "What work?"

Instead of telling me that I had done it wrong, Mr. F talked with me for a while. He started by saying that the way I did it was a wonderful talent. He really tried to understand how I approached the math—that when I see a problem, I also see the answer. I had no clue that other people took little steps to get from the question to the answer. Instead of just telling me I was wrong, Mr. F explained that it was important for me to learn what steps other people take because someday I may have a new concept in math, and I would need to be able to speak the language to explain it to other mathematicians. Also, he said that even I would eventually get to a level of math where I had to take some steps.

Mr. F spent a lot of extra time that semester helping me to understand about taking steps. And because he explained the need so thoroughly, I didn't feel that he was trying to make me slow down or to do it "his" way for no good reason. It was hard to learn what steps other people take, but over the next few years I found out just how indispensable it is to understand about taking steps.

—Boy, 15, North Carolina

**I have a shining example of a gifted teacher. In third grade, instead of assigning research on one of an approved list of barnyard animals, Ms. S asked me to come up with a topic I would like to study. I got to spend over a month reading books on quantum physics. Wow! I will never forget Ms. S!**

**—Boy, 16, North Carolina**

My BS-o-meter clues me in to the gifted teacher. They don't make things up to compete with the students. They say when they don't know something instead of turning the tables back on you for asking a question. They also are willing to throw their hands in the air and acknowledge when their teaching isn't working.

—Girl, 16, New Mexico

**Someone who gives trust, and gets it in return by treating students as human beings with complex lives—and lots of emotions because we gifties are very deep.**

**—Girl, 17, New Jersey**

The ability to control our eccentricities.

—Boy, 17, Washington

**A case of dry erase markers that smell like fruit, a wry smile, a playbook of witty sarcasm, the ability to steer a topic in 19 different directions, a strong sense of imagination, and passion about something.**

**—Girl, 18, New York**

# SCHOOL IMPROVEMENT

Listen to most any politician, school board member, or business leader as they evaluate the educational system. In much of their rhetoric you will hear that schools—especially in the United States—are behind other countries in test performance and preparing students who are "college or career ready" when they graduate from high school. It seems that schools (especially teachers) are under constant pressure to push students to ever higher levels of performance.

We decided to ask the people with the most at stake in the schooling process—students like you—what their thoughts were about appropriate change strategies for improving education. As you read through these comments, see which ones apply most to your current school situation. Also, consider a conundrum that many educators face today—"How do we prepare students for future jobs that don't yet exist?"—as few adults seem to agree on how to accomplish this important task.

## YOUR TURN

Imagine you have been asked to serve on a local school committee to select a teacher for a newly formed gifted program. Part of your job is to generate a list of characteristics and/or skills the successful candidate should have.

What personal *and* professional qualities would you require the candidate to have? Why did you choose the attributes that you did?

If you were lucky, and you had multiple candidates who were in the running for the job, which three qualities would be most important to use to narrow the candidate pool?

What one quality would "make or break" the job offer to a candidate?

## How could school be improved?

Honestly, I have so much frustration in school that I find it hard to come up with suggestions. I suppose the only way is to create a classroom for the top 10 or so children in each grade. Otherwise, the best thing to do is to find another learning environment where you can meet other students like yourself and meet teachers who understand you and respect your ability to learn.
—Boy, 13, New York

**Teachers could give us different spelling words. I mean, would it kill them to come up with more challenging words than "stocky" and "diagram"?**
**—Girl, 13, Ohio**

I'm in the last grade where we have a GT program. Next year I am expected to pick courses in high school that will challenge me, but I have so many interests that don't match any specific classes offered. I can't take AP courses yet (you have to be a junior at our high school), and there are no electives for GT students. It is a veritable no-man's land for the next year or two. I feel lost and no one seems to care. How about an elective course for GT kids so we have a place of comfort we can grow from into the high school environment? I don't think that is much to ask.
—Boy, 13, Florida

**Instead of focusing on making students sit still and passively absorb information that doesn't interest them just so they can pass tests, teachers can try to get students to actively participate. Most of all, I *never* want to hear a teacher say (and I have often heard this), "Oh, you don't need to learn that because it is not on the test."**
**—Girl, 14, Illinois**

In elementary school, I would always get very excited when I spent a day with people like me. There are special education programs for students who learn slower than others, and I think there is no excuse for not having a similar program for gifted students.

—Boy, 14, Ohio

**I love being challenged, but sometimes, I just want a break, which I can't have. Last Wednesday was the first time I can remember in 2 years when I had no homework due the next day.**

**—Girl, 14, Washington**

Teachers could have us get to know other students like ourselves more so that we can have people to relate to. I mean, we should still be able to hang out with other kids, but I don't feel that I know many other gifted people.

—Girl, 14, Maine

**Teachers could better enforce rules against cheating and bullying.**

**—Boy, 14, Massachusetts**

Less review and more assignments that actually involve thinking.

—Girl, 14, England

**High school credit for online courses I complete because they are interesting. I just about have an associate's degree done on my own, but can't get the degree because I'm "just" a high school sophomore. Does this make any sense to you?**

**—Boy, 15, Georgia**

Give me the work, theory, idea, and then let me run with it and figure it out for myself for a while.

—Girl, 15, Iowa

Let me choose at least one area of interest for me to study. Let me choose what books to read. Let me move at my own pace. Don't find me busywork to do while everyone else catches up. Don't expect me to go slower to stay with the group.
—Boy, 15, North Carolina

# YOUR TURN

### Special Programs for the Gifted

Special programs for gifted students have always been controversial, with some people seeing them as a necessary part of a school's operation and others seeing them as elitist. Some are one-day-a-week pull-out enrichment programs with a teacher trained in the characteristics of gifted kids and in methods of providing an educational haven where it is safe to be smart. Others are full-time self-contained classrooms or even magnet schools where an emphasis is placed on providing curriculum that challenges and propels gifted learners to reach for the stars.

As you read through the following comments, consider where *you* stand on the issue of providing special programs for gifted students. Should they exist or not? And if your answer is yes, how would your gifted programs be structured for the various grades (elementary through high school)?

Should schools provide any programs for gifted students? Why or why not?

Should there be something at the high school level (other than AP options) for gifted teens? Why or why not?

Also, project a few years ahead and consider if you would want your own child to participate in a gifted program. Why or why not?

Let's add some humor to classrooms. In my gifted program, we are always laughing, cracking stupid jokes, and doing stupid things. It's wonderful.

—Girl, 15, Oregon

**Don't give kids the idea that it is okay to be mediocre.**
**—Girl, 16, Illinois**

Forget grade levels. Don't try to force your concept of socialization on me. If you put me with other students who are basically kind and at my academic level, I will appear to you to be a properly "socialized" kid. If you put me with bullies or kids with lower abilities, I will appear to avoid contact with my classmates, and you will put labels on me that are unfair.

—Boy, 16, North Carolina

**I would like to see more schools exclusively for gifted students, schools that employ only teachers who are committed to their jobs and treat students like responsible people. I would make these schools accessible to low-income families like mine.**
**—Girl, 16, Indiana**

I would suggest putting us in smaller classes so we could learn at our own rate. Also, get rid of those time-consuming standardized tests.

—Boy, 17, Michigan

**A clear pathway to college when you are ready to go, not based on high school completion or class membership. My junior year has been spent on all electives because I exhausted the curriculum already, and I have another year to go!**
**—Girl, 17, Wyoming**

When you ask most teens—gifted or not—what their passions are in life, you seldom get an answer like "fifth-period geometry." Even if you love math so much that you dream in numbers, your passions for math probably go way beyond what is included between the covers of a textbook. The same is true whether your passion is in music or theatre or geology or video game design—your passion grows from someplace inside of you.

The Green Econ Chick you're about to meet in the following essay knows full well how to both identify and nurture a passion (or, in her case, multiple passions). Read along and digest her insights.

# Ikya Kandula
## Confessions of a Green Econ Chick

I think the number one thing I learned throughout my years here at the Davidson Academy, a Hogwarts-esque school for gifted students, is to *get involved*! There is really no other way to put it. You need to put yourself out there, push yourself beyond your previous limits, and believe in yourself.

I got involved with the Green Earth Community Knowledge Organization (GECKO) because I had never really learned much about environmentalism and, with my newfound interest in just about everything, I really wanted to see what it was all about. I attended the first meeting, then the second, and then the third. Before I knew it I was president. Somewhere along the line, I realized how interested I was in sustainability, energy conservation, and environmentalism.

I was beginning to find a niche, but the cool thing about a niche is that it can involve more than one interest. I mean, obviously, people aren't just into one thing nor do they have one hobby. You can personalize your niche like you would your bedroom. Go on, throw in those band posters, glow-in-the-dark stars, and pink streamers.

I wanted to explore a little bit more, so in the second semester of my freshman year in high school, I decided to take a university marketing class to learn more about business. I wasn't completely satisfied, so the next semester, I took a microeconomics class. I realized I was interested in business and economics, especially behavioral economics.

I started meeting with my professor; founded the business club, DECA, at school; and took a bunch more university-level classes. I looked into undergraduate business programs and kind of fell in love. I even named Wharton University's undergraduate business program as "My Crush" on my bookmarks page!

I found my niche. I discovered my "thing." I was a Green Econ chick.

This doesn't mean I'm only interested in just environmentalism and economics. I have many, *many* interests. I like sociology, Harry Potter, yoga, and food. I plan on going to a school with a strong undergraduate business program and doing research on behavioral economics. I also plan on pushing for change in my community so we can be more environmentally conscious. I'm even currently working on a project to get apartments in Reno (NV) engaged in recycling (more than 2/3 of the major apartment units in Reno don't recycle!). All in all, I'm getting involved, doing what I love, and loving what I'm doing!

*Ikya Kandula is a 16-year-old living in Reno, NV. She plans on studying behavioral economics in college and saving some trees along the way. She hopes her advice, although simple, will resonate with others and help them accomplish their goals.*

# SUMMARY

From boredom to community activism, this chapter allowed you to experience school from many varied perspectives. We even prompted (nudged?) you to think about school from the "other side of the desk," putting you in charge of hiring a teacher for a position in gifted education.

Some of you saw something in these pages that resonated with your school experience. Others likely realized school can be a very dynamic experience—much more dynamic than your current experience suggests.

In any case, we hope you recognize that activism and involvement are key to success. You do have much more potential to guide your school experience than you might believe. Whether they are happy times or horror stories, school will provide you with memories that last a lifetime. And if a little personal creativity gets into the mix, all the better.

Now, get out there and get involved!

# chapter 5

# FAMILY LIFE

**THEY** come in all sorts of sizes and combinations. They cause or share in your highest highs and lowest lows. They provide the context and backstory for your most heart-wrenching and hilarious tales.

We're talking about families, and whether they are biological, nuclear, extended, or in a constant state of flux, everyone has at least *one* of them.

Our families tell the stories of our lives. Taking time to hear these stories and reflecting on their underlying messages uncovers insights about who we *are*, who we *were*, and who we might *grow to become*. If life has a foundation, be it weak or strong, it is often this thing called "family."

As a teen, you are stretching to extend contact with the world, and in many ways moving beyond your family in doing so. This time can be stressful on everyone, especially if you have been an active member of your family unit. As you become more

## YOUR TURN

Consider this. Did you ever wonder where those sitcom writers got their story matter?

independent, more involved in making your own decisions, and less reliant on your parents and/or siblings for encouragement and direction, the dynamics of your family may change. And this change may not always be appreciated by those who have loved you since birth!

This chapter gives you the unique and rare opportunity to see inside other gifted teens' family lives. Some of the stories shared might resonate with you, while others seem so far-fetched that you believe they could only have been borrowed from *Family Guy, South Park,* or *The Simpsons.*

## What has your family said to you about being gifted? What are their expectations of you?

My parents expect me to do well and study hard. I think my mother is scared of the genius stereotype.
—Girl, 13, Massachusetts

**Being gifted is a great responsibility. I'm supposed to act as a role model for my siblings—but my 16-year-old brother gets excused for being a dork because "you know, he's not gifted like you." I mean, *really*?**
**—Girl, 13, Kentucky**

My parents never talk to me about being smart. Most of the time I get the feeling that they just don't care.
—Girl, 13, Kentucky

When they found out I was gifted, my parents didn't react at first. Then, after they talked a while, they called me in and told me we were going to try a few doctors to get a second opinion.

—Boy, 13, Pennsylvania

**My parents have many times talked to me about my special talents. I seem to accomplish in everything I do, and they realize this. They talk with me about many things, and they encourage and love me. My parents and I have a very good relationship.**

**—Boy, 13, Kentucky**

My parents do not believe that I am gifted, merely that I am somewhat bright. I refute this notion. I consider myself to be gifted, and I work as such to gain the deserved recognition.

—Girl, 14, Australia

**Even though I am smart, it is hard to keep up with the standards my parents set for me. They tell me that I am smart, yet I am still struggling to keep my grades up.**

**—Boy, 14, Oklahoma**

They have said that they are very proud of me and they expect me to be the best in everything I do. I'm not sure what to think about that last part.

—Girl, 14, Ohio

**Because of my giftedness, my parents have said a great deal to me. They say that I must be a role model for students in lower grades. They also dictate that because I am gifted I must strive for a better and harder education than the normal curriculum offers. I feel that being a role model can add pressure to a mind that has already been compressed with a load of very hard and long work due to a very strict, high-level curriculum.**

**—Boy, 14, Texas**

Every time I do something wrong, my parents remind me that I am gifted. My parents forget the fact that being gifted also means being creative. I only wish that was the characteristic my parents would see in me the most.

—Girl, 14, Missouri

**My parents are always talking about me being gifted and how different I am compared to other people my age. They tell me how lucky I am to be smart and that I should never be ashamed of myself or anything I do. They expect my grades to be in the 90s, and they also expect me to do the right thing when I go to places like parties or movies.**

**—Boy, 14, Texas**

My parents say that being gifted will get me far in life and that I have to appreciate it. They don't think of me as a child but as an adult who is just smaller than they are.

—Boy, 14, California

**They often say, "Don't embarrass us by turning into some sort of bookworm. Play sports, get dirty outside and enjoy yourself. There will be plenty of time to test out and exercise that brain of yours in your life."**

**—Boy, 15, Alaska**

Because of my abilities, my parents expect me to be very responsible and to always keep my grades high. I sometimes feel they have asked me to grow up faster than normal. I just wish they wouldn't have such high expectations for my future. They tell me they just want me to be happy, but at the same time feel that is only possible by engaging in high-paying, high-prestige careers.

—Girl, 15, Iowa

**Since I am a gifted child, my parents said that I should compete with myself to be the best that I can**

be. They also said not to worry about the others. They expect me to get good grades, but an occasional C is okay with them.

—Boy, 15, Arizona

I sometimes think my mom is sick of my good grades. Sometimes I catch her saying, "Can't you just make a C once in a while?" (I don't even know if I could if I tried.)

—Girl, 15, Indiana

They expect me to do great things in life. The hard thing is that none of them seems to be able to tell me what these great things might be! They say I'll figure it all out, but I'm not so sure.

—Boy, 15, Louisiana

My parents always tell me that I can do better (like I haven't heard this enough!). They also expect me to have common sense and to use it, forgetting that I am a teenager and that teenagers do stupid stuff.

—Girl, 16, Pennsylvania

When I was little, like 2 or 3 years old, they always told me that everyone has gifts—maybe being a good listener or running fast or whatever—and that my gifts were being good at reading and math. I also knew I was good at making babies happy, and I liked doing that, so I include that as one of my gifts.

—Boy, 16, North Carolina

## YOUR TURN

The responses in this section show a wide variety of adult reactions when it comes to their child's giftedness. Which ones sound the most like your parents' reactions? Which ones sound least like your parents' responses? If you become a parent and have a gifted child (or two) to raise, what do you think you will tell him or her about being gifted?

My parents go on and on about how I should make a 98–100 percent in every class, graduate as valedictorian, go to West Point, serve in the military, and get a really high-paying job. It drives me crazy because, yes, I want to do those things, but not to the extent that they want me to. They don't see me getting married and having children. They see me in a huge house, probably by myself, with enough money to support them when they get old.

—Girl, 16, Georgia

**My dad says I should strive to have people work for me instead of me work for other people. Mom says to be kind and helpful, to give back. I say to get my car fixed and find a girlfriend.**

**—Boy, 17, Wyoming**

My parents haven't really said anything to me about being gifted, though I wish they would. I don't think my father is gifted, so I guess I can understand why he wouldn't be very comfortable talking about giftedness with me, but my mother is gifted, and I wish she would talk about it more often. I always felt out-of-step emotionally and intellectually with my classmates (even those in the gifted program) and I never knew why. I researched giftedness on my own and was surprised (and relieved) to find that my feeling of being different was related to my giftedness. I never knew how much being gifted colored a person's entire self. No one ever explained to me that a lot of my social/emotional difficulties and peculiarities came from being smart.

—Girl, 17, New Jersey

**My parents merely say that God granted me a gift and not to let it go to waste. They don't really expect anything of me, for they "know" I will go on to be successful in life.**

**—Boy, 18, Tennessee**

My parents expect me to be the first in our family to graduate from college before getting married and starting a family. I want a bit more out of life, though. I want to travel and earn an advanced degree in international banking so I can get away from this rural life.

—Girl, 18, Washington

**My parents don't talk to me unless I'm in trouble.**
**—Boy, 18, Alabama**

They have always been proud of my accomplishments and helped me not overreact to my failures. They always say being gifted is a challenge to find your life's calling and to provide for those less fortunate by giving something back. Being gifted requires solving problems, not just complaining or blaming others for them. They expect me to be humble and honest, but to never compromise my ideals or morals.

—Girl, 19, New York

If you've ever had to endure wearing a pair of shoes that was two sizes smaller than your feet, you know how uncomfortable that feels. All you want to do is toss those shoes across the room and let your toes wiggle in unbridled glee! Well, Santiago Gonzales knows that uncomfortable sensation, not because his shoes were too small, but because his school curriculum was. What you'll pick up from Santiago's story is that the best solution to an educational dilemma is to take your case to some adults—including parents—who can lead you down new paths where you can walk in total comfort.

# Santiago Gonzalez
## Cogito Ergo Sum

When 14-year-old Santiago—Santi—Gonzalez wakes up at 5:30 a.m. each school day, he spends his first waking hour developing applications for his iPad. Following this mental exercise, he barnstorms his parents' bedroom just before their alarm rings. Then, after completing his requisite tooth brushing and breakfast rituals, Santi and his mom head out for the 30-minute drive to his classroom—at the Colorado School of Mines in Denver, where Santi is a sophomore. Having started his higher education experience at Arapahoe Community College at age 11 (taking courses in Genetics and Flash Animation), Santi is now a full-time student at one of the nation's most respected schools of engineering. Santi's professional goal? To work at Apple as a product developer.

*Cogito ergo sum,* "I think, therefore I am," is more than just a cool Latin expression; it is also the mantra of Santi's life. But things haven't always been so great for Santi when it comes to his education. Let's look at Santi's journey through his schooling—the good and the bad—and investigate how a kid whose age screams "middle school" but whose mind savors "valence shell electron pair repulsion theory" has made the educational system adjust to him, not the opposite.

Santi's parents, Vanessa and Yago, moved to Colorado from Mexico City when Santi was still an infant. When Santi had memorized the alphabet by 18 months of age, and could count to 20 in three languages by the time he was two, they realized that preschool for him would need to be a tad different than typical. The Montessori school he attended let Santi be Santi, allowing him to explore fractions at age 4 while other kids his age were digging in the dirt or playing with blocks. For bedtime stories, Santi had two preferences: Winnie-the-Pooh and nonfiction books on natural history, where he became fascinated with rocks and minerals to such a high degree that he turned the family laundry room into a crystal-making lab.

Kindergarten was equally as enjoyable for Santi's absorbent young mind, as his exploration of the natural world progressed from rocks and minerals to astronomy, where he became fascinated with the big bang theory of cosmic creation. All of his intellectual burners were being lit by both his school and his summer experiences. Life was sweet, both in school and out.

Until first grade.

The regimentation of a classroom that required simplistic reading and math assignments confused Santi. School was supposed to be a place where you learned stuff. For him it was more like a twisted prison where his dreams were squelched and his abilities ignored. Even recess became a chore, as Santi's 6-year old classmates didn't care much about the distinctions between igneous and metamorphic rocks. Given this daily ritual of intellectual and social mediocrity, to Santi, not being "normal" . . . was becoming normal.

In search of answers to explain their son's abilities, Santi's parents had his intellect tested. Not surprisingly, Santi scored far beyond the range that most kids his age attain. A private school for gifted kids was the answer—at least for a while. Although Santi was placed in a third- and fourth-grade classroom at age 7, the so-called "advanced" curriculum was still not sufficient. Luckily, Santi had a teacher who was inventive and not intimidated by Santi's obvious intelligence. Those 3 years gave Santi a place to fit in, at least better than before. Sadly, though, Santi's next teacher's style didn't complement Santi's learning styles, and things fell apart once again. (Santi recalls that this teacher was "like a vacuum that didn't suck well." Pretty useless.) That's when Arapahoe Community College entered the picture, as Santi was admitted based on his entrance exam scores, not his age. Not long thereafter, the sympathetic chair of the computer sciences department at the Colorado School of Mines interviewed Santi and his parents and suggested that Santi attend there full time.

Which brings us up to the present day: Santi has a full schedule of university classes each semester, from Chemistry 2 to web development, to Calculus 3 and software engineering. He typically sits in the front row in his classes and is not afraid to ask his professors to answer questions or to elaborate on the theoretical or practical implications of their lectures' content. When he completes his bachelor's degree in computer science and math at age 16, Santi then plans to pursue two master's degrees (computer science and electrical engineering). He considered doing a Ph.D., but believes that working for 4 years on just one topic wouldn't be something he would enjoy.

Socially, he is pretty much on his own at school, but when Santi returns home, he enjoys playing soccer with his younger sister,

Andrea, and getting together with his extended family for his weekly addiction, watching *The Simpsons*.

*Cogito ergo sum*. This phrase is an apt description of Santiago Gonzalez, a young man whose intellect and imagination have finally been allowed to soar to their natural and intended heights.

We were lucky to speak with Santi and understand his story, but for a fuller description of Santiago's educational journey, we encourage you to read "Santiago's Brain," by Jeff Tietz, which appeared in *Rolling Stone* magazine on December 8, 2011, pages 78–87.

Do adults in your family ever brag
about you or compare you to others?
If so, how do you feel about this?

I sometimes find my parents comparing me to my brother, who is also gifted. I do like to hear the compliments, but I don't like the comparison because we are two different people and I sometimes feel that I need to live up to his standards.

—Boy, 13, Michigan

**I used to think "so what?" when it came to compliments, but now I have really learned to listen and appreciate compliments, as I then put forth more effort. Compliments kind of make me smile—like a hug does. They sneak up on you and surround you to protect you from anything bad.**

**—Girl, 13, Kansas**

One day I found out that I had gotten first place in the math competition and had gotten a trophy. That day, when I got home, my mom went straight to the phone, dialing the first number that came to her head. She then called every relative we have, including those in Dallas and Mexico. She did this for a whole day. Talk about embarrassment!

—Girl, 13, Texas

**My parents brag about my good grades all the time. My mom makes sure that everyone she works with knows about my awesome intelligence.**

**—Boy, 13, Texas**

My parents brag and compare me to all the other kids in our town all the time. When I was little, it felt good to be noticed for being special. As I have grown and spent more time socializing through Facebook, I see that my accomplishments pale in comparison to other kids out there. I'm worried my parents are in for a big letdown about their little girl!

—Girl, 13, North Dakota

**When I hear my parents (and sometimes even my sister) talking about me and making comments about my good grades, I feel embarrassed and I blush. But later, when I think about what it is that they were saying, I feel so good about myself that I want them to keep bragging about me!**

**—Girl, 14, Kansas**

Sometimes I hear compliments that feel hollow. Like when I get a good grade, but know that I didn't do much work. I know my parents know it too. But how do you argue with the grade of A?

—Boy, 14, Maine

**My parents never brag on me. They have said several times after hearing other people brag on their children that everyone is different and has different interests and strengths. They say the world is too full of competition, and I should just focus on being me and being happy. What a relief!**

**—Girl, 14, Maine**

I have caught my parents talking about my abilities or comparing me to my sister. Sometimes, my sister overhears these conversations, and she feels really, really bad, because she thinks she is not good enough. I hate when they do this because she is not old enough to be compared to my abilities.

—Boy, 14, Arizona

**No, they really don't brag about me. They make sure I know they are proud of me, but without exploiting me. My brothers were not as blessed as I in giftedness, but they have talents that I do not have, especially in thinking mechanically. In this way, we have**

all felt as equals and were very blessed to grow up in harmony with each other.

—Girl, 15, Iowa

I feel that it is not fair that parents compare you to someone else and not to yourself. They don't understand that it is hard to match up to anyone else. They want you to become someone else that you are not.

—Boy, 15, Colorado

**My parents used to brag about my high grades and caring disposition all the time. That changed when I became a high schooler and my brains took a backseat to my hormones.**

**—Girl, 15, Mississippi**

I don't mean to sound conceited, but it would be nice if every once in a while I did hear my parents brag about me.

—Girl, 15, Texas

**I have heard my parents answer questions about me, which I guess could sound like bragging, but mostly, they are just being honest. (Boy, THAT sounds like bragging by me, doesn't it!)**

**—Boy, 15, North Carolina**

Sometimes I feel proud that they think so much of me, but other times I get tired of it and just want to be thought of as a regular person. I sometimes feel pressured to do exceptionally well in some things just to please my parents.

—Boy, 15, California

**Yes, they compliment me, which feels nice, although the compliments are unnecessary. I am other things besides smart.**

**—Girl, 16, Indiana**

I don't have brothers or sisters to be compared to, but I do catch my parents, especially my dad, bragging about me. It makes me feel kind of awkward, because I don't know how to react.

—Boy, 16, New York

**No one in my family is compared to anyone else— we're all in this thing together.**
**—Girl, 16, Ontario**

My parents do compare me to other successful kids but they never brag. I think they used to, but remembered what it was like for them growing up. They are more of a support structure for me than anything. I like that they are behind me and help me make decisions.

—Boy, 17, California

**Brag? No. Complain about and compare? Always. I feel like I can't quite ever do enough or be enough. It is totally frustrating. I quit sharing what I'm doing in college to get some peace. When is "good" good enough? Never, to my parents.**
**—Girl, 17, Maryland**

Compliments? No time for those. My parents regularly nag me about not working up to my capabilities.

—Boy, 18, Kentucky

**They don't really compare me to my sister because she has a learning disability and so that wouldn't really be fair. They have compared her grades to mine if she does better than I do. I think they do this to encourage her, but it still annoys me.**
**—Girl, 19, Oklahoma**

Now that I'm away at college living my dream, I miss the good-natured prodding my parents used to help me be my best. It was an odd security being prodded to not settle for mediocrity. At college, all of us are [the] "best of the best" which means I'm now about average, but of the best. I could use a hug and a prod to put in a little more time and effort every so often.

—Girl, 20, Connecticut

# YOUR TURN

Many places in this chapter provide a tongue-in-cheek look inside the rites and rituals of family life. One of America's most beloved satirists helped many families overcome the stress and (seemingly constant) aggravation of family life. Her name was Erma Bombeck, and her irreverent way of sharing her family life amused thousands. Below is a typical quote from Bombeck about family life.

The family. We were a strange little band of characters trudging through life sharing diseases and toothpaste, coveting one another's desserts, hiding shampoo, borrowing money, locking each other out of our rooms, inflicting pain and kissing to heal it in the same instant, loving, laughing, defending, and trying to figure out the common thread that bound us all together. ("Erma Bombeck," n.d.)

Use the above sample as inspiration. Satirize family life based on your experiences—or use some poetic license to create a fictitious account of family life that is sure to amuse others. (Remember when we talked about creativity in Chapter 4? Tap into that rich vein of creative energy you have and enjoy!)

What has your family done to get you interested in new things? What haven't they discussed with you that you think they should?

There are college-level biology, chemistry, and physics books lying around—and they are heavily used. In our home environment, everyone debates the validity of new medical research and everyone is expected to ask questions.

—Girl, 13, New Jersey

**Ever since I can remember, it has been the library, the museums, the park programs, repeat. We are a family in constant motion. I wish they would ask me now what I'm interested in before making arrangements for *every* program.**

**—Boy, 13, New Hampshire**

My parents need to talk to me about boy-girl relationships, because I'm about ready to have one!

—Boy, 13, Michigan

**My dad always talks about his job as a nuclear engineer since I find it interesting. I love to listen to him talk about anything because his voice is so quiet and soothing.**

**—Girl, 14, Ohio**

When I was little, they introduced me to sports and let me choose whatever sports I wanted to go into. I like that.

—Boy, 14, Texas

**I do feel, and I am quite embarrassed to say this, but I think they should talk to me about sex. I feel that could clear up a lot of my questions.**

**—Boy, 14, Arizona**

So far, my parents haven't done anything to get me interested in new topics. The only thing they do is tell me to study harder. I think they're afraid I will lose my GT title.

—Girl, 14, Texas

**I sit down with my mom and watch the news. She'll discuss things with me that I don't understand. (She explains things very well, in my opinion.)**

**—Boy, 14, Connecticut**

My parents pretty much leave me alone. But they try subliminally to introduce me to new things. For instance, out of nowhere my dad has taken an interest in the Nature Channel and clicks over to it from sports when I sit down near him in our living room. I've begun asking him about engineering, medicine, architecture, chemistry, and forensics just to see what he'll do next!

—Girl, 14, Wisconsin

**They really haven't done anything. All of my research and extended interests were of my own volition and motivation.**

**—Boy, 15, Iowa**

I wish they would talk to me more about making friends, because I suck at this. At this point, I think I've missed out on the whole adolescent social thing.

—Girl, 15, Indiana

**I grew up in a Catholic family, but I wish they would have pursued religion more than they have. I want to go into depth with my religious study, but I hardly know where to begin. I have a lot of questions that no one seems to be able to (or want to) answer. It just isn't enough for me to go to church on Sundays.**

**—Girl, 16, Iowa**

My parents have been really great about letting my interests guide what we do. They are supportive of almost any idea I have come up with wanting to try. (I'm glad they did pooh-pooh the opera singer thing though.) I wish they would talk to me about careers and girls. I need to figure out both before I get too old for either.

—Boy, 16, New York

**My parents really don't do anything to interest me in new topics, aside from clipping a newspaper article or getting me a book. However, they don't prohibit me from being interested in anything. (I'm not exactly sure how they *would* prohibit me, if they had the mind to do that.)**

**—Girl, 16, Pennsylvania**

My parents should discuss all the reasons I should have unlimited funds for video games (that's a joke). Honestly, I can't think of anything they should discuss but haven't. Sometimes they insist on discussing matters I wish they'd avoid (homework and bedtimes), but that's about it.

—Boy, 16, North Carolina

**We travel to unique destinations a lot. My dad says I need to be aware of lots of places, customs, and people to be successful in life. I guess my parents encourage me to try new things by always doing this themselves. Our family life is one adventure after another. I think it is great.**

**—Girl, 17, Nevada**

My parents tried to introduce me to new things when I was younger, and I appreciate that. They should have introduced me earlier to theology and philosophy, but another relative helped me to discover more about those topics.

—Boy, 17, Kansas

**I wish my parents would have taught me about how to discuss difficult issues with people. I am really caught**

up in some emotional issues about my choice of a major here at college, but I don't know who to talk to or how to even start a conversation. I feel stuck. HELP!
—Girl, 18, Colorado

## YOUR TURN

Make a list of activities, topics, or situations that you would not have been involved in were it not for your parents' influence or intervention. Next, list those activities, topics, or situations that your parents *forced* you to try or consider. Lastly make a list of activities, topics, or situations that you pursued *despite* your parents' objections. In comparing these lists, consider which items resulted in the most memorable or significant experiences for you—and which ones were memorable for all of the wrong reasons (that is, you gained little from them.) Do you notice any trends as you consider the source of your best and worst life experiences?

Much of this chapter has revolved around exploring what family members do and say to gifted teens. We chose this approach to help you gain some understanding about how your family does impact the person you are (and are becoming). But, we don't want to end this chapter on such a clinical note.

Finding joy and happiness in life is often not much more complicated than recognizing what you already have and the simple pleasures of living in a constantly changing world. In this last section of the chapter, respondents tell us what makes them happiest at home. And guess what? It's often pretty simple stuff.

## When are you happiest at home?

Love from my family is what makes me happiest. When I say "love," it means so many different things such as just caring for me and supporting the things I do.
—Boy, 13, Ohio

**The Internet is a crucial, absolutely crucial, factor in my life. Being mentally connected through chatrooms, instant messages, message boards, and common fields of interest and similarities in personality is absolutely necessary to me.**
**—Girl, 13, Australia**

When I have really stressful days at school, I like to go home and just kick back. Even though that never happens, I try to imagine it like it did. I get so overwhelmed with having so much to do when school is done that being inactive makes me happiest at home (at least in theory).
—Girl, 13, Texas

**I love when my dad and I are doing everyday activities, like walking in the woods, watching TV, or just asking him a question I have about science or math. As a joke, we write on little strips of napkins or newspapers lots of equations to solve. I clearly remember when dad asked me to name 10 ways to measure the height of a building with a barometer when I was 7. And just recently, we calculated vectors while watching *Fear Factor* reruns.**
**—Boy, 13, New Jersey**

Easy—my Beats® and time to just sit in a chair with my eyes closed and relax to the drive of the newest alternative rock I can find.
—Boy, 14, Indiana

My sister makes me happy because she is really silly, and I need that. She is almost 3 years older than I am, but since I'm gifted, I can understand what she is talking about.

—Girl, 14, Ohio

Just coming home to a nice clean house with no drama makes me happy. It makes me feel as if my household is peaceful even though I know we have problems like any family.

—Boy, 14, Iowa

My brother makes me very happy. It was a hard year of adjustment when my brother moved out to go to college. Suddenly, I didn't have my confidant anymore. I guess it was a good thing, though, because it forced me to make friends that I wouldn't have otherwise.

—Boy, 15, Minnesota

I feel guilty saying this, but my boyfriend makes me feel happiest when he is around. He is a college freshman and is not superbly intelligent, but since he is older, he is at my maturity level. He is my best friend. I feel like I can talk to him, and he doesn't judge me for being young or smart. He makes me feel good about myself.

—Girl, 15, Indiana

We have always had cats since I can remember. They are wonderful "purr"veyors of fuzz therapy. If you are ever feeling down, bury your face in a cat's tummy as it purrs and see if you don't feel better!

—Boy, 15, North Carolina

At home, I like to do something I can do nowhere else: Have time to myself. To relax, play with my pets, jump on the trampoline, or just listen to music.

—Boy, 16, New York

What makes me happiest at home is music. Whenever I go home, I always listen to music, whether it is classical, hip-hop, or Mexican. For me, it creates another world that I just escape to. It can also inspire me when I do a project for school. Some of my best projects have come from that.

—Boy, 16, Florida

My music and books make me happiest. I love to play, write, and listen to music, and read good books with detail and suspense. These are my only ways to get away from people who are always telling me that I need to work harder.

—Boy, 16, Georgia

I'm happiest at home with my dog. He doesn't want anything more of me than to rub his tummy, feed him, and give him lots of love.

—Girl, 16, Pennsylvania

I'll paint a vivid picture—keys to the car, money for pizza, an Internet café with a few friends to play Gears of War live, and the brunette cheerleader who hangs out with her friends drinking latte watching me from a distance. If I could only get up the nerve to repaint this picture to change the last two pieces [I'd be] spending time with my brunette girlfriend [and] drinking lemonade (I don't do latte!)—priceless!

—Boy, 17, Idaho

The thing that makes me happiest at home is when I have a chance to just relax and do something silly—or even babyish! When I can take an afternoon and read children's books, watch a video of a TV show I loved when I was little, color in a coloring book, or snuggle up with my favorite dolly and a nice, warm blanket, I am very content. I guess that's a little pathetic, but it makes me feel good inside because it's pressure-free, allowing me to just let go of all the responsibilities and worries that go along with being 17 years old.

—Girl, 17, New Jersey

The happiest times at home are when my entire family sits down to our Saturday dinner. It is an absolute requirement for everyone to be there—no exceptions. It is a crazy time, but each of us gets to catch up on our family life, which brings me back to a state of calm belonging. At home, I fit in and am no different than anyone else. We're all a little weird in our own unique ways, and it is totally accepted.

—Boy, 18, Florida

**My sister makes me happiest at home. She doesn't really care how I do in school, and so we can just relax and have fun. I don't ever have to worry about her looking at me in a different way.**

**—Girl, 19, Oklahoma**

Now that I am away from home more often than there, the happiest thing is that I am totally accepted for the person I am and mostly only the good things about my life. There are no pretenses or personas you have to have or show at home. It is nirvana. But, just for a while, until I lick my wounds from life and get back out there to make more mistakes or accomplishments in the rat race of living as an adult.

—Girl, 20, Vermont

# SUMMARY

We mentioned at the introduction to this chapter that family provides the foundation for a teen's developing life. After reading the many stories and experiences shared, perhaps a better analogy would be that family is "the calm that counters the chaos" that is most everyone's daily life.

In this and the previous chapter, we tried to allow teens to share how they fit within the common life experiences of family and education. Your personal story might mirror very closely some of the situations you've read about. Indeed, you might have unwittingly found yourself in these pages. Or, you might now be wondering how and why your life story is so vastly different than those shared within these pages.

We have only provided representative experiences in this book from the many thousands of individual stories that exist. Your story is unique, and we expect it varies in ways both big and small from the ones we highlighted. Unique and different are good. Your story and life experiences are vintage you!

The tide now shifts from an exploration of the present and past to a look toward the future. We've encouraged you in previous chapters to keep looking forward and to keep your dreams alive. Let's take a "bird's eye" view of your developing self.

# YOUR TURN

**Unplug to Reconnect With the World**

Daily life is very complex. Parents often are all working, teens are involved with extracurricular activities and perhaps their first jobs, and younger children are linked through social networks to people across their city and the country. Regardless of the setting, the expectation is that you are connected and available through some device at all times. Very little opportunity is present for recharging or building close connections on a live personal level (this means face to face—not using Facebook or Facetime!).

Getting outdoors and away from schedules and responsibilities is a great way for families to connect. Think of three outdoor activities you can do with your family in the next week. Here are a few examples just to get you thinking: Take a walk in the park; go camping (even in the backyard!); ride your bikes around the neighborhood; play flashlight tag after dark; build a fire, make s'mores, and tell ghost stories; play a game of baseball or soccer—without keeping score; go sled riding; take a canoe trip down a local river; and so on.

Talk these options over as a family, choose one, and do it. Afterward, ask each person to answer the following questions on paper, then sit down and share results.

> ➤ How did doing the activity make you feel?
> ➤ What did you like and not like about the activity?
> ➤ What should we do next?

# chapter 6

# A LOOK TOWARD THE FUTURE

You have brains in your head.

You have feet in your shoes.

You can steer yourself

Any direction you choose.

—Dr. Seuss

THEODORE Geisel, otherwise known as Dr. Seuss, had a way with both words and ideas. Using simple rhyming lines, he managed to address some of life's most complicated issues using uncomplicated language. And along the way, he made us both laugh and think.

In the book quoted above, *Oh, the Places You'll Go!*, Dr. Seuss wants his readers to know that life can take you in many directions—and that many of them are good. It's the same with lots of gifted teens we know: They are smart enough to become just about anything they choose for a career, yet they are overwhelmed (or, at least a bit confused) by the wide array of interesting possibilities from which to select. So, if you love both the arts *and* the sciences, do you become a doctor or a dancer? If economics has always been of keen interest, but video game design seems equally as engaging, which do you choose? And why? And how do you decide? If these scenarios sound familiar to you—join the club. Selecting a career path when so many are available and appealing to you is a condition so common among gifted teens that it's even been given a name: multipotential. As you read sections of this chapter, you'll find lots of company in your quest for that perfect job.

Something else you'll read here is whether or not gifted teens are hopeful for the future—their own and our planet's. In a world that seems beset with problem after problem, pain after pain, do our world's most intelligent teens feel more optimistic or pessimistic about what lies ahead? Read on, read on . . .

One certainty about your future is that there are no guarantees. Life is funny that way: its most important choices often have no clear-cut paths to success. Too, when an opportunity or challenge comes your way, you might wonder if it's worth your effort to push ahead. In reading this chapter, both the student comments and the Your Turn activities, we hope that you get a bit more clarity about what your future might have in store for you—and what you might do to direct your own course. Just remember: "You can steer yourself any direction you choose."

Cloud computing and the intellectual property rights issues that are bound to come from open sharing of data and development of programming.

—Girl, 13, Alaska

I often wonder whether being immortal would solve the problem of having to choose a life specialization, but it is a useless wish. Instead, I'm going to learn as much as I can about everything from multiverse and string theory to animal and plant form and function. Also, prosthetics is amazing and a topic of interest, especially the mechanical and electrical engineering aspects of it. Biophysics, oceanography, and pi are also high on my list. There is simply not enough time!

—Boy, 13, New York

Right now I'm working on novels written in verse.

—Girl, 13, Ontario

I want to learn French. I haven't had time to take French because I'm in band in middle school, and we only get one elective.

—Girl, 14, Texas

Technology so I can program and invent, not just use it. I want to know how and why technology works, not just that it will make my life easier. As far as I can tell, technology makes life more complicated, complex, and confusing—not easier.

—Boy, 14, Alabama

**I would like to learn more about the past, not necessarily U.S. history. We just read a book called *The Devil's Arithmetic*, which was about the Holocaust. I'd *really* like to learn more.**

**—Boy, 14, Michigan**

How the subjects we take in school actually mix together in life. I'm tired of being told I'll need such and such in the future. I want to know how such and such impacts my life now, not some time down the road.

—Girl, 14, South Dakota

**I am interested in the political and religious systems of other countries. Of course, we never talk about these in school.**

**—Boy, 15, Indiana**

I want to learn about pitching in baseball. It's all physics, trajectory, and velocity, so I ought to be able to figure out how to do it well.

—Boy, 15, Virginia

**Law, because it leaves me in awe. Even though some people can't imagine a 4' 10" girl being an attorney, I can!**

**—Girl, 16, Indiana**

I'd like to learn how to study in different ways. I am starting to have some trouble in organic chemistry and don't know what else I can do to learn better. Memorizing just isn't working for me anymore.

—Boy, 16, New York

## YOUR TURN

If you could choose any person, living or dead, which historical, literary, musical, athletic, or other individual would you like to share a dinner with? Why? What would you talk about? What would you hope to learn from this person?

I am absolutely fascinated with autoimmune diseases. Particularly, I would like to find out why Raynaud's phenomenon happens and find an effective way to treat it.

—Girl, 16, Pennsylvania

I'd like to learn how to be more accepted and fun in public places. I know I am smart but feel really dumb when it comes to socializing.

—Boy, 16, Virginia

I want to learn about outer space and the deepest depths of the ocean.

—Boy, 17, Tennessee

About the real lives of inventors. How they got someone to actually buy their invention and how to market ideas. I'm just clueless about this process, and I can't find info online.

—Girl, 17, New Jersey

I want to have hands-on experiences in hospital emergency rooms. Not just a biology course, but the real thing.

—Boy, 17, Oklahoma

Eastern religions and philosophies, as well as advanced physics, are of most interest to me. It's not usually lack of time, but lack of people in those areas to talk to or learn from.

—Boy, 17, Nebraska

How to make an informed decision would be near the top of my list. I just roll with a decision and often end up in a pickle. Better decision making in the beginning sure would save a lot of time and aggravation.

—Girl, 18, California

How to be decisive and more sure of myself. I can often see how many possible solutions could be right depending on the situation. This causes me to seem confused or disorganized to others. It's no fun weighing all the options in a microsecond and not being able to pick a course of action.

—Boy, 18, Texas

# THE "P" WORD

Potential.

This is a word gifted teens hear a lot. We even used it a few times in previous chapters. (*We told you it would be a recurring theme!*)

For many, hearing what others think about *their* potential can leave them feeling a little nervous. If you are working to it, what can you expect in the future? If you aren't working to it, people quickly challenge your giftedness or point out that they are wondering if you are destined for laziness and a less-than-successful life.

If that sounds like you, take a look at what one former gifted teen—now a gifted adult—has to say about the pressure of potential. KaSandra, age 19, has been through the same thing.

I was often told that I could do or be anything I wanted because I was so smart. But I had a hard time figuring out what this really meant. It ended up meaning to me that if I didn't get all A's, act sweet and agreeable all the time, and have loads of friends, I was letting my family down. It took quite a while for me to overcome the stigma of potential in my life.

But KaSandra did get over the worries that came from potential and expectations and learned to make decisions for herself. "You cannot let other people's expectations decide for you what you should do," she says. "You need to use your emotions along with your intellect to help guide you toward a career destination."

## YOUR TURN

Does having potential leave you feeling a little nervous? What does this term mean to you? How do (or would) you define potential? Why do you think other people focus on it? How does this externally imposed focus impact your life?

## What are your future plans?

To achieve. To know. To learn. To grow upwards. To explore the full range of my abilities. To write. To express. To discover. To impart. To teach. To communicate.

—Girl, 13, England

**I want to become a Federal Air Marshal and then earn my pilot's license.**

**—Boy, 13, Ohio**

I am going to become a grade school teacher, because I love to help little kids. I want to teach them basic stuff about school and life. I'll be a teacher my whole life until I retire when I am *really* old.

—Girl, 13, Texas

Right now, I want to be a bone doctor or a journalist. It's funny that there is hardly any relation between the two, yet I still want to be both.

—Boy, 14, Maryland

Well, I'm just going with the flow right now, so I'll figure it out in high school. I like doing makeup and hair, I like writing mysteries, and I love to cook. So . . . we'll see!

—Girl, 14, Tennessee

**I'm working toward a career in the NBA. After that, I'll be a sports analyst on ESPN and have a side job as a chemist.**

**—Boy, 14, South Carolina**

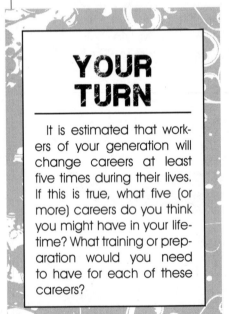

## YOUR TURN

It is estimated that workers of your generation will change careers at least five times during their lives. If this is true, what five (or more) careers do you think you might have in your lifetime? What training or preparation would you need to have for each of these careers?

I have plans to be a physical therapist or teacher, and one of my nonacademic goals is to go parasailing before I am 21.

—Girl, 14, Louisiana

**My future plans are to finish college and get a good job. I don't want to get pregnant until I am ready for a crying baby.**

**—Girl, 14, Texas**

I want to be a paperback writer. Maybe I'll write a book you'll want to read!

—Boy, 14, Connecticut

**I'm not sure what I want to major in yet, perhaps law or engineering or aerospace technology. Or perhaps elementary education. After that I will live alone until I feel I have my life completely started. Then, I'll settle down and be an active part of a small community.**

**—Girl, 15, Iowa**

When I get to college, I want to study aeronautical engineering. During some point in my life, I want to be a professional tennis player. That's about it for right now, but I'm sure I'll add a lot more plans in the future.

—Boy, 15, Arizona

**Since I am very interested in eyes, I would like to study to be an optometrist. Who knows, though? Maybe my mind will change in a few years, so my backup plan right now is to become a lawyer.**

**—Girl, 15, Colorado**

Professional snowboarder, where I can shred the mountain all day and then spend my off time shooting commercials and traveling. This way I get to see the world and will have a nice bank roll tucked away for when I'm old in my 30s.

—Boy, 15, Oregon

**I want to get married during college, and then study to become a high school English teacher and later a school administrator before I retire.**

**—Girl, 15, Indiana**

I really have no idea what to become. Every time I consider a career, it is always shattered by the reality of the job and how much school the profession entails.

—Boy, 16, Wisconsin

**First off, I am not going to grow up. I may get older and wiser, but responsibility will be something I pay other people to have for me. I will move from career to career and be a smashing success at anything I do. Thanks, Mom and Dad, for the great intelligence you passed on to me. And, for the support you share when I have a crazy idea and you tell me to "go for it."**

**—Girl, 16, Rhode Island**

I plan on making my money early in life. Then, I'll enjoy myself and have fun. I plan on avoiding as much of life's grief and sorrow as I can by being independently wealthy and wise.

—Boy, 16, Nebraska

**Since my family doesn't have much money, I will not be able to go to a college that is not near home. I have set my standards and goals extremely low, I'm afraid.**

**—Girl, 16, Texas**

I plan on taking life as it comes at me. Trying to plan too much just sets you up for failure and high anxiety. I'm not into the whole rat race thing.

—Boy, 17, Nevada

**After years of working as a psychiatrist, doctor, lawyer, or engineer, I want to be able to retire and enjoy my grandchildren and spoil them while traveling a whole lot with my loyal husband.**

**—Girl, 17, Virginia**

I'd like to go to a really good school in hopes that there will be other gifted people like me there. If I don't go to college, I may work in construction or perhaps take up a craft or trade. I'm really not sure. If all else fails, I would like to be a street poet in San Francisco.

—Boy, 17, Kansas

**It worries me that I don't have a clear plan in sight. I hope to start college, but have no idea what to major in. There are so many careers that intrigue me, but you have to pick early, and how do you know what your life work is supposed to be when you are 17?**

**—Girl, 17, West Virginia**

Many gifted teens possess "multipotential," which we described earlier as the ability and interest to perform a number of careers with equal (high) success. You might have picked up on this ability through the future plans shared in the previous section.

Although multipotential can be seen as an asset, it can also be a burden. It is hard to know exactly what it is you'd like to spend your life doing. This is especially the case when you can see yourself doing disparate, but interesting things, based on your many passions.

Many gifted people not only have complex minds, but complex and intense emotions, as well. It's not that they are clairvoyant or possess magical powers, but they are able to see beneath the surface of what people are saying or how they are acting to get to the core of their beings. Richard Schild is one of these young men. As you'll read, Richard's mind is always racing forward with new thoughts about his current passion—engineering—but his heart is keeping pace with his mind. It is this convergence of intellect and emotion that makes Richard—and many gifted teens—the complex, intimate characters that they are.

## YOUR TURN

If you are afflicted with multipotential, is it more of an asset or a burden for you? Why? What steps can you take now to explore several career options to help you make a more informed decision about which career(s) to work toward?

# Richard Schild
## Focused on Passing the Present

I'm Richard Schild, a mechanical engineering student from Karlsruhe, Germany.

I started taking computer science courses at university while still a gymnasium [high school] student. I was at least 6 years younger than the other university students. But, I performed well—even though my gymnasium teachers tried to hinder me from attending university classes. They would have liked it if I had participated in competitions as a gymnasium student because it is easier to deal with pupils doing things you "already know" rather than dealing with pupils going other ways.

I felt cheated by this and looked for other educational options. I applied for and received a scholarship to a Jesuit Boarding School—even though attendance meant I needed to skip grade 10 (the scholarship was for 11th grade, but I applied and received it as a ninth grader and had to grade skip to take it—my second time grade skipping—to be able to attend).

It was at this time (I was 15 years old) that I discovered I had an ability to "read" people rather precisely by observing their actions and making a little conversation (about 2 minutes or so) with them. I did this intuitively, by paying attention to the way they behaved, answered questions, and by what they *did not* say. I never "trained" to observe people, and it does not work with people I'm emotionally interested in (like my girlfriend). But, I am typically very accurate with my judgments.

This ability does cause some concerns for me. With peers, the things I usually discover are their problems—especially if they are trying to hide them from others.

Because I have a strong feeling of "duty to look after others," my intuitions often lead to uncomfortable discussions. If you get that someone has a special problem, and you know roughly what kind of problem you are encountering, then it's usually easiest just to ask the other person and have a conversation about it. Sometimes these conversations are very emotional. So, I try to limit this dimension about myself to try to stay happy.

On a positive note, this intensity made me more compassionate. I did volunteer work in Belgium with patients having disabilities and mental illness. It became much easier for me just to let people do the things they do without judging how strange these things are after having insights into other people's disabling conditions and behaviors. I learned to be much more tolerant and nonjudgmental. This was important because it helped define my character.

I know there are other people that share this intensity to read others. I wonder how they see it—as a chance, a duty, or a bad thing, and whether they ever want to get rid of it? For me, the emotional side of it causes a lot of personal concern and conflict.

Currently, I am pursuing a degree in mechanical engineering and hope to turn this into a dual diploma program with study abroad in France. In Germany, mechanical engineering is a classical job. But, engineers work everywhere, not only where you'd expect.

I was accepted for a law degree program but found that without some logic, mathematics, or an equivalent, my mind was getting soft—like an athlete not doing sports or a musician not playing his instrument or listening to music.

In the end, I want to do something that helps people. Not necessarily like UNICEF, but maybe protecting them in a better way, reducing the amount of energy they need, or something like that. I think science cannot solve all problems—but it can solve many!

As for computer science, which was an early passion, the more I learned, the more I realized that there are "race conditions"—unforeseen errors just there, but possible to reconstruct without immense work—that spoil the fun. And, it's not that easy to be creative because it is not the way I like to think. I enjoy focusing on moral and ethical issues, which are too complex to be adequately pursued with computer science at present.

The other problem is that the technology changes so fast most of your energy is spent trying to stay caught up and specializing to survive. I realized that computer science was not what I wanted to do in life.

Looking to the future, in every case, I want to continue social engagement through science. Concerning "life and career"—I'm not sure. Principally, the thing I appreciate and I hope most for in the future is to find people who are a bit like me and understand me. Right now, I'm just a little focused on "passing the present"—looking after the future when it comes time to do so.

Richard Schild, 19, is studying for a degree in mechanical engineering at the Karlsruhe Institute of Technology (one of the leading universities in science and engineering in Europe) in Karlsruhe, Germany, and hopes to soon be dually enrolled in either the diplôme d'ingenieur en génie mécanique or l'école polytechnique in Paris, France.

As a 50-year-old, I'll probably reflect back on something I built as an engineer. I would have probably built something that revolutionized the automobile industry. I might also be reflecting on a time when I caught a huge fish. Of course, I don't know what the future holds for me, but I hope it is mostly good things.

—Boy, 13, Texas

**I solved Fermat's Last Theorem, collected my million bucks, and moved to the South Pacific and enjoyed my life of fame from my bungalow on stilts over a turquoise sea.**

**—Girl, 13, Georgia**

Unfortunately, my life took a strange detour leading me to become #3 on Interpol's most wanted list. I found a way to hack any encryption code and had access to all the world's secrets and finances. I now travel the globe in total secrecy, and my wealth is unending.

—Boy, 14, California

**I hope by then that I have helped at least a thousand people and not charged them anything. I just want to look back and see that I have helped people better their lives.**

**—Girl, 14, New Mexico**

I lived life large and learned that paparazzi destroy your privacy and ability to be a regular human being. I wish I could have kept one of my seven wives so I would now have company instead of all these alimony checks to write. Life is lonely when you are at the top.

—Boy, 15, Massachusetts

**I can't do that. I don't want to. There's so much I want to do—everything in fact. I want my life to be a continual surprise.**

**—Girl, 15, Illinois**

I had fun times, hard times, and sad times, but I stuck through it all the way.

—Boy, 15, Iowa

**After college graduation, I moved away, purchased a home with my husband, adopted a few children, and opened my own school for gifted children. At 60, I moved to Florida and became a golf junkie.**

**—Girl, 15, Indiana**

My first 50 years were spent unraveling the genetic code and finding a means of delivering eternal youth to humans. Heading into my next 50 years, I hope to settle down and start a family.

—Girl, 16, New Hampshire

**I'd like to think I was the all-time leader in strikeouts in the Mars Baseball League, did a lot of interesting and cool stuff in computer science and math, and maybe even had kids of my own. No, that's too weird. I can't imagine 50!**

**—Boy, 16, Arkansas**

I went to college as the young African American woman that I am. I got over every obstacle that blocked my way, and I worked hard to become a successful doctor.

—Girl, 16, Michigan

## YOUR TURN

Do you think issues like high expectations, perfectionism, or boredom will go away or become easier to deal with as you get older?

Of all the obstacles you currently face as a gifted teen, which one(s) do you think will linger on beyond the school years? Which ones are likely to be resolved (or reduced) after high school or college graduation? Why?

**I'm not sure what I will have done, but I hope I will be proud of whatever I accomplished and the choices I made.**

**—Boy, 17, Wisconsin**

Our family is my greatest accomplishment. Our six children are just beginning their adult lives, which is wonderful to watch. Fortunately, my last three novels have become runaway hits and the trilogy will hit the big screen soon. Life has been good so far, and I can't wait to finish my current writing project!

—Girl, 17, Pennsylvania

**I have retired after 20 years of serving my country in the U.S. Air Force. I have a wife and three children, and I regularly explore the world, for its secrets are endless.**

**—Boy, 18, Tennessee**

I might die before I am 50. This makes me want to cry.

—Boy, 18, Alabama

Are you hopeful about the future?

Yes, but I will have to get a little organized.

—Boy, 11, Louisiana

**With new technologies, despite the chaos it might bring, the world will be a better place in the future because of a few strong individuals. Physically, emotionally, or intellectually, these people will grasp onto ideas to better the world. I hope I can be one of those people.**

**—Girl, 13, New Jersey**

I live as an optimist. Without hope, what is there in life?

—Boy, 13, Washington

**I am not hopeful because we are still all going to die. Yes, I dream and wish for some things, but overall, cynicism is safer.**

—**Girl, 13, Ontario**

It depends on what you mean by this question. If you mean *my* future, then, yes, I am very hopeful. If you are talking about the *world's* future, then my answer is no.

—Boy, 14, Connecticut

**I do feel hopeful about the future because I have a lot of support in my life. Also, I always do everything to the best of my ability, and I think that quality is going to help me. My parents support me a lot and that motivates me to have positive ways of thinking about my life. I have hope because I believe in myself and others believe in me.**

—**Girl, 14, California**

I always say, "When bad comes, there is always good behind it," because you can't go through life dwelling on the negative. You'd be miserable.

—Girl, 14, Ohio

**I don't think life will get better or worse. Every day is the same for me.**

—**Boy, 14, Massachusetts**

Every door I come to is open, and while that is a little scary, I know I'll make the right decisions when I need to.

—Girl, 15, Iowa

**I have this theory that if you think of the worst, that's how things are going to work out, so I always think of the best.**

—**Boy, 15, Illinois**

I wonder sometimes why adults can't seem to solve problems or at least sit down and talk things over. We are constantly told to play nice with others and respect differences. Yet, these same goals are often totally ignored by adults. This leads to wars and other negative outcomes that impact everyone. How is this so difficult to see from the adult perspective? Yes, I am hopeful, but that hopefulness gets chipped away every time I see an adult or our government make a stupid decision based more on emotion and pride than intelligence and wisdom.

—Girl, 15, Wyoming

**Am I hopeful? So much so that I believe the Cubs will win the World Series next year, or maybe the year after that, maybe.**

**—Boy, 15, North Carolina**

Hope helps me make plans for the future. It is the hope that my life will be a good one that carries me through each day. Hope also is a coping mechanism that leads you to change your ways in order to better fit your ideal sense of being a person. Yes, I am a hopeful person—a romantic, some would say.

—Girl, 15, Utah

**My friends make me feel hopeful because they're good people with the same high standards I have. With God, my parents, and my friends, there is nothing not to be hopeful about.**

**—Boy, 15, Texas**

The future is what I live for—I can't wait! I know it is going to be great!

—Girl, 16, Indiana

**The only way forward is through a sense and belief in hope. Think how depressing life would be if you gave up on your hope for anything better. As I see it, without hope, you are an empty shell of a person, probably destined for life in prison or worse.**

**—Boy, 16, Wisconsin**

I can't really say that I feel hopeful about the future in general. I find myself quite disgusted with the way society is today, and I think that can only worsen over time. Overall, people are ill-mannered, uneducated, and overly dependent on technology. All people seem to care about is careers, dieting, and being sexy. I often wonder if people remember how to *think*. If I could, I'd start my own world from scratch. Most days I think that the one we're on now is messed up beyond repair.

—Girl, 17, New Jersey

**Being secure in my abilities and potential, I know I will succeed.**

**—Boy, 17, Tennessee**

Living in a small town in the rural Midwest has really drained a lot of hope out of me. I doubt that I'll marry, and I'm not sure I'll be motivated enough to make it through college.

—Boy, 18, Nebraska

**I am a hopeful person. This helps me see past the nose on my face and my immediate life circumstance toward a future that is brighter than my current situation. It might be scary to see so many possibilities and not know which one is the right one for me. But, it is better to have options and hope than to rely on the [chance] that you will win the lottery by spending your last $10 to try to change your life.**

**—Girl, 18, Florida**

Many teens in this section express a strong sense of hope for the future. They expect the future will lead to a better life. Some would say these individuals have a lot of resilience and a positive outlook on life. Others might say that the rough realities of life's struggles will teach these gifted teens some life lessons that are sure to bring them down a notch or two.

We believe a sense of hopefulness is what carries us forward in life. Dream big dreams and live your life based on your sense of hope for the future. Tie your passions to your sense of hope and you'll have a powerful mindset in place— a sense of passionate hopefulness.

## YOUR TURN

Have you identified areas in life where you are passionate about getting involved? What are some of your ideals (or hopes) for your personal future? Do you have a lot of hopes or just a few? Which are the three most important to you? Why?

What can you do to inspire a deeper sense of hopefulness in yourself? In others?

## Career Paths . . . Living Your Dreams

We all want our life dreams to come true, and we tell ourselves that we are going to try our hardest to attain them. But the truth is, most of us don't reach our highest dreams, and we settle for something lower. But I don't want to "settle." Once I pick a career, I'm going to try and try until I accomplish what I want.

—Girl, 15, Ohio

**I cannot fathom a single professional career. My dream is to be able to prepare for multiple careers cutting across multiple professions. I think this way I**

**can follow my interests and also can count on being flexible enough to always have a job. This is a looming worry for me. How do you prepare for a future where the jobs are likely to be very different from the present; perhaps the jobs don't even exist yet? And, how do you know if your dreams are going to match what the future holds?**

**—Boy, 16, Washington**

My dreams and hopes for the future are constantly changing. I have not found a pattern to life that gives me the ability to focus my efforts and prepare myself for a career. I am afraid that I'll make a choice that requires a lot of training and then find out near the end of my preparations that my interests have changed yet again! How do you pick a career path? How do you know that you have chosen the right one?

—Girl, 17, New York

**I have always been told to just go for it. But I cannot decide what things can hold my attention for the rest of my life. I am at the cusp of adulthood but I don't feel at all like I can be an adult. The responsibility to choose wisely now, so I have a successful and fulfilling life, paralyzes me. I am accumulating credits and it is time to pick a major or career path. I don't know what to do. Can you help?**

**—Boy, 19, Massachusetts**

You should have asked for advice about matching your dreams to a successful career path. I need some help in deciding how to channel my many interests into a meaningful career. I would like to be independent and financially able to raise a family one day soon, but I don't want to close doors on options at this point in my life. I want it all, but can't even decide what all really is.

—Girl, 20, Florida

# YOUR TURN

What dreams do you have about your future career path?

In an earlier Your Turn activity, we pointed out that the future likely holds several career changes for you. Hey, if you have to change, you might as well have a plan, right?

Fold a sheet of paper down the center ("hot dog bun" style). In the left column, list careers that (might) interest you. Once you have completed your list, rank your top five from most interesting to least interesting.

Spend some time online researching the amount and type of training you need for each of your top five careers. In the right column, list the training requirements for each of your top three careers.

Compare/contrast your interest in the career with the training requirements. Has your interest changed based on what you have learned about training requirements? Has your top five career list changed?

Can you find a person who works in each of your top three careers to talk to about his or her experiences? What advice do they have for you? Can you do a job shadow for a day? (Ask! They will be flattered and probably very willing.)

When you try to pinpoint what it is that makes one person successful while another one with equal talents or skills is less successful, there is no magic formula. Some might say it is "being in the right place at the right time" or knowing someone who can get you that perfect summer internship or entry-level job. However, these are more elements of chance than they are directions you can follow. Is there anything that *you* can do *directly* that might increase your likelihood of life success?

Well, according to Zoltan Mesko in the following essay, the best person to determine your future is . . . you. And the best ways to ensure success have more to do with getting actively involved than with hanging back passively. As you'll read, this formula is working very well for Zoltan.

# Zoltan Mesko
## The Symbiotic Relationship I Found Between Academics and Athletics

My education began in former Communist Romania. I grew up in a city of 300,000 called Timisoara, where four languages are spoken: Romanian, Hungarian, German, and Serbian. Before I knew it, I was fluent in the first three of these languages. I attended a school where everything was taught in German. School in Romania was absolutely grueling to me and my classmates, for along with having to learn high school level mathematics in elementary school, I also had to deal with memorizing a different lengthy German or Romanian poem almost daily. The catch to this was that we were cold-called to recite it in front of the classroom—there was no escape! It was tough to manage my academics, along with having to go to polka dance rehearsals (yes, laugh it up, my mom's at fault on this one) but with hard work, I got through and did well in school.

In 1997, my family received wonderful news that we had won the U.S. green card lottery, something that millions of foreigners apply for every year. Only 55,000 families annually get the privilege of coming to America to pursue their dreams, and we were fortunate enough to beat the odds.

When I first enrolled as a fourth grader in Queens, NY, learning came easily to me. I did struggle with English initially, but I became fairly fluent in just a couple of months. Within the year, I had caught up to everyone in reading, writing, and spelling, but I was studying the same math that I had learned in second grade. Because I wasn't being challenged in math, I became complacent, because it is in our human makeup to take the path of least resistance.

One of the catalysts that really started my development as a student, an athlete, and most importantly, as a person of character, was my teachers' realization that I needed to be challenged more. This got me placed with the gifted students in sixth grade. To cope with the increased level of difficulty in school, I started to play soccer for the local travel team and basketball at the local YMCA (obviously, I had more skill in one sport more than the other, but I refuse to tell you which!). I found sports to be a great escape from becoming overwhelmed or burnt out by school. However, it is important to note that the opposite also proved true. I had found a unique symbiotic relationship between the books and the sports arena. I like to call it my "developmental ying and yang."

When I moved to the city of Twinsburg, OH, in seventh grade, the same formula kept working and my development kept progressing. Eventually, I graduated from high school with a nonweighted GPA of 3.97, and my $45,000 per year college tuition was paid for by my ability to play football. Once again, and on a much grander scale, athletics had helped out my academics. The academic side was what I had always banked on, and if football was going to be a vehicle to help me get my college degree, then so be it.

I never intended for my athletic skills to earn me a living, but with hard work and that symbiotic relationship between the books and the sports, that's exactly what happened. I figured that if my football career didn't work out, my enrollment in one of the top five business schools in America surely would. After graduating, I ended up staying an extra year at college and earned my master's degree in sports management.

The benefits and life lessons I learned as a student-athlete *throughout my schooling* are absolutely priceless. The skill set I developed by having to juggle multiple commitments taught me more in life than anything else.

I strongly encourage anyone to follow a similar path. I'm not just talking about getting involved in sports, but you have to do something else other than academics to keep you going—something that truly makes you tick, something you're passionate about. Play an instrument, sing in the choir, volunteer, dance, act, join the science or chess club. Just get out there and have something that will make you constructively forget about your academic stresses. Doing so diversifies your risk and complements your development. When you do something legitimate and productive in your free time (which you'd otherwise waste playing video games or twirling your thumbs), you will undoubtedly recharge your "academic battery," too. Consequentially, you will enhance your overall development as a human being.

One other thing I'd like to address is the effort and sacrifice it takes to become successful. The one lesson I learned more through sports than anything else was the formula and habit of hard work paying off. It was easier to see this through sports than academics, because the results were immediate and apparent. However, I started realizing that the "hard work formula" applies in every aspect of life.

I have never considered myself a super-intelligent person, but I believe that I worked harder at tasks than many around me—I've definitely stretched my envelope to its fullest. I really pride myself on the sacrifices and countless hours I've put into any daunting task I was assigned by others or that I assigned to myself. At the end of the day, when the grueling hours of studying and dedication to something I love are through, the suffering completely dissipates and I embrace my reward. Remember this: Things that are worth your time are going to require both hard work and sacrifice.

I love it when I run into someone and they give me the usual excuse of "Oh, but you are smart and talented and things come easily to you." First off, I tell them they have it completely upside down, as the reasons behind my success are hard work and determination more than anything else. Second, I quote one of my favorite Teddy Roosevelt lines: "I am only an average man but, by George, I work harder at it than the average man."

We can't change the cards we are dealt, but we can certainly control the way we play them. Play yours well.

*While playing football at the University of Michigan, Zoltan Mesko earned his bachelor's degree in finance and marketing as well as his master's degree in sports management. He is currently a professional football player with the New England Patriots (and played in Super Bowl XLVI), after having been drafted in the fifth round out of college.*

# SUMMARY

We opened with *multipotential* in this chapter and end with *reflection*. Your life requires an almost continuous cycle of identifying opportunities, making choices, and reflecting on your decisions. Some people believe they have little chance to mitigate what they might call fate and give in to their perceived lot in life. Others take a more proactive position, continually scratching and clawing toward making their dreams into reality. These approaches are extremes, and chances are good you will be of a middling sort. But, regardless of your perspective, reflection is a key component to your knowledge, understanding, and developing wisdom.

Looking toward the future is as much an emotional endeavor as a developing plan of action. There are choices to be made without enough information to feel comfortable or foresee an outcome. There are also curve balls that life will throw that you cannot hope to hit.

All in all, the journey and brief respites you take to reflect on things are key to discovering and developing your own map from here to the future. Maybe cartography should be one of those five careers you are destined to encounter throughout your life. Do you have an interest in sextants?

Get busy charting your course!

# chapter 7

# QUESTIONS AND ANSWERS ...SORT OF

There is nothing deep down inside us except what we have put there ourselves.

—Richard Rorty, American Philosopher

IN this chapter, we present a mélange of themes and activities meant to address questions that concern gifted teens, but didn't quite fit within the parameters of the preceding chapters. Most of the ideas presented come from a simple, but profound question:

Is there anything else you would like to share or know about being gifted that we haven't asked about?

In the sections that follow, we'll attend to some of the themes tossed out by gifted teens based on the aforementioned question. We'll use a few actual responses to introduce the discussion. In some cases, we'll share answers from teens or young adults we know. In others, we will just give you the opportunity to "sit with" the idea or question and wonder about how you might respond.

As usual, we also give you more opportunities to explore your personal giftedness with Your Turn boxes. After all, this book is meant to help you make some sense of the "G word" for yourself!

Skip around in this chapter, if you'd like. The topics are introduced with no particular intent or order in mind.

# PASSIONS, PEERS, AND COLLEGE

I wish you would have asked how others found more gifted kids like themselves. Even with most of my good friends, it's hard to relate to them.

—Boy, 13, Massachusetts

If you agree with the standard definition of giftedness being the top 3% in any population, it does make sense that a gifted person would be at a big disadvantage in happening upon another individual that fits the category of giftedness. For instance, in a high school class of 100, there would be only 3 of your classmates who would qualify according to the standard. Now, take into consideration individuality, and, you can see how difficult it might be to find a like-minded other who also shares your interests or passions!

Here is what we learned from Zoe (age 12, California) about how she found other people who share her passion:

I have always had a passion for musicals. I have lots of musicals on CD and like to see them onstage to know what the actors are doing when singing. My favorites are *Les Miserables* and *Wicked*. I was so enthralled with them that I learned piano at the age of 4 so I could write my own compositions to turn into musicals.

This passion for musicals in particular was a real problem when it came to making and keeping friends. Very few of the kids I met when I went to school even knew what a musical was. And, the few who did had only seen either the *Wizard of Oz* or *Seussical the Musical*. There was very little depth to their knowledge. They were kindergarteners, so what should I have expected?

This was very troubling to me. I felt completely alone in the world at the age of 5. Fortunately, I was able to do some work in our local community theater group. The story behind this experience is the real interesting part, though.

My mother volunteered herself as a performer in our local community theater group and just included me as part of her practice routine. I loved going to rehearsals and mimicking the different parts that actors were practicing on the stage. I realized later that my mom did this to find a way to support me. She really had no intention of ever performing on stage!

After seeing me acting out my mom's part while she was on stage, the producer asked if I would like to try out for a small part. The rest, as they say, is theater history. At the budding age of 5, I was a performer on stage.

I found friendship with many of the community theater people through my passion to perform, not my age. I was, in some cases, decades younger than my acting peers, but that didn't seem to matter to them. We shared a love for the stage, and this made everything right. My mom was even okay with being cut from the production, even though I was included in the cast.

My advice is to get involved in your interests and take some chances in life. You might not find many, or any, age mates who share your interests or abilities at school. So, you'll need to get out in the real world and find a way to feel good about yourself.

Your parents can help if you are young, and if you look at your local paper, you might find a way to involve yourself and find friends who share your interests, even if they don't share your age.

Get involved in your passion area. Find a way to do something that makes you feel good about yourself. Friendships develop from the sharing of similar interests, and you'll see that age really doesn't matter all that much.

—Zoe

I want to know how other teens found friends and acceptance when they went on to college. I worry now that my close circle of friends is breaking up (as we head to different colleges) that I won't find anyone I can relate to. Is this a common experience? How do you overcome it?

—Girl, 16, Michigan

Ah, college. This exciting (yet nerve-wracking) time in your life is when many teens find themselves and their passions for the first time. And, every other freshman feels the exact same sense of anxiety and confusion that you do! You get a fresh start to remake yourself—if you want—while having the seeming luxury of making your own decisions and living on your own. Curious to know more about this side of college? Just read the following essay. It's funny. It's accurate. You'll learn something.

# Chad Gervich
## On Going to College

On the first day of my freshman year at Vanderbilt University, I showed up wearing denim overalls. Although overalls were the hottest thing to hit my Iowa hometown since hot pants and leisure suits, little did I know that they had gone out of style in the rest of the world a couple of decades earlier. There I stood on the brink of adulthood, away from parents, teachers, curfews; ready to face new challenges, obstacles, and responsibilities . . . and I looked like Opie Taylor (son of Sheriff Taylor, as in *The Andy Griffith Show*, for those of you who don't watch old sitcoms).

Not that it mattered. Away from the cliquishness of high school, friends were no longer chosen on the basis of wardrobe, appearance, or how fast their cars could go.

College's greatest attribute may be its tolerance level. Because most colleges boast a spectrum of students of all nationalities, income levels, religions, colors, sexual orientations, athletic abilities, races, interests, political affiliations, heights, widths, weights, depths, fragrances, genders, and cultures, people look beyond these incidental traits when choosing friends. College has a niche for everyone. It is your responsibility, however, to find your own niche.

The most important two words in creating a successful college career are *get involved*. No one ever made friends while sitting alone in a dorm room, and as exciting as Molecular Biology 101 may be, the heart of the college experience lies not in classes, but in friends and activities.

Most colleges, at the beginning of every year, have some sort of organizations fair, where all of the campus clubs, groups, and associations set up booths for interested students. Don't miss it—and sign up for everything. Even if you don't have time for 216 extracurricular activities, you'll get a lot of e-mails and texts, and your friends will think you're really popular. You'll find organizations for writers, readers, artists, artsy people, people named Art, athletes, scholars, athletes who date scholars, athletes with scholarships, scholars with ships, scholars with lips, lippy people, Mick Jagger fans, people who fan dance, line dancers, dance majors, military majors, military protestors, protestors who protest protestors, animal rights protestors, party animals, animal lovers, animal crackers, people who crack up easily, easy-going people, people with fleas, people with trees, tree-huggers, people who like hugs, and virtually any other social organization imaginable. There's an outlet for everyone.

Sign up for more extracurricular activities than you could ever possibly handle. The busier you stay, the less of a chance you give yourself to get bored or homesick. Ninety-nine percent of bored or homesick kids haven't allowed themselves the opportunity to make friends or find extracurricular activities. Although you may not ultimately commit to every group on campus, you'll make a ton of friends simply by meeting people. The more things you do, the more people you'll meet, and the more friends you'll make. And in the process of sampling several organizations, you may stumble across something new and exciting.

The best way to find study time is to allow a few hours each day (yes, *each day*) when you can sneak off and be alone. If you can get into a pattern of studying at the same time and place every day, studying becomes painless. Try to find a secret hideaway where you won't be bothered by the commotion of campus life: a special corner of the library, an old desk in the dorm basement, a table in a deserted classroom. Avoid places like the 50-yard line or the middle of the student union's Taco Bell.

The more you organize your days, the less stressed you will become. In addition to study time, schedule time for exercising, going to classes (duh), texting friends, and even goofing off with your buddies. As you grow more accustomed to your day's schedule, you will find free moments when you can be spontaneous, but your schedule acts as your guide.

If you're having trouble with homework, get in to see your professor as soon as possible. Make an appointment with the professor's secretary or go in during office hours. Usually, professors love helping students and most of them enjoy getting to know their students on a personal level (not *too* personal, however). Relationships with professors can develop into lifelong friendships. Also, most of them have friends and contacts around the world, so they're great when it comes to pulling strings at graduate schools or for job interviews and internship possibilities. Professors can also be great at writing letters of recommendation or lending a hand at many other life-determining crossroads.

Contrary to what your high school chemistry teacher tells you, college is not all that excruciating. Although college is meant to challenge you, it also offers you the means to tackle those challenges. Open the door when opportunity knocks, and don't be afraid to taste samples from the great collegiate smorgasbord.

You only get one shot at college, and despite the long view as you move into your freshman dorm, 4 years whip by amazingly fast.

College has a place for everyone; you simply must find yours —even if you're wearing overalls.

*Chad Gervich graduated from Vanderbilt University and then received a master's degree from UCLA, majoring in creative writing. He has written and produced on television shows such as After Lately, Reality Binge, Malcolm in the Middle, Girls Club, and Wipeout. The author of the best-selling book Small Screen, Big Picture: A Writer's Guide to the TV Business, Chad lives with his wife and young son in Los Angeles.*

# LONELINESS VERSUS ALONE TIME: WHAT'S THE DIFFERENCE?

Some people believe that gifted individuals are more prone to loneliness and depression than others, as there are not all that many people out there who are gifted like you. Others feel just the opposite: that being gifted opens up your choices of people with whom you can communicate, thereby limiting loneliness more than in a person of average intelligence. Below are some gifted teens' thoughts about loneliness.

Lonely? No, I have lots of friends and even when I can't contact them, I still have myself. Depressed? Why be depressed if I can live my life to the fullest?
—Boy, 13, Florida

**Sometimes it is hard. I feel awkward talking about how I feel lonely because I know the topic of gifted-ness will arise, which will make me sound egotistical and/or melodramatic, which I don't want to be. That would estrange me even more from others.**
**—Girl, 13, Pennsylvania**

No, I have some adult friends who are capable of talking at my level. Besides, I've only felt a limited desire for socialization, as I prefer the company of my books, my poetry, and my land.
—Girl, 14, Nebraska

**Nah . . . I can make a whole world up in my mind. How could I let the fact that I am alone in my thoughts make me feel bad? I imagine a lot, and this imagi-nation will be my ticket to fame and fortune.**
**—Boy, 15, Oregon**

Your thoughts on the issue might align with any of the previously mentioned beliefs. Loneliness can be debilitating and depressing if you let it. But, there is another take on the issue for some gifted teens (and adults). The sense of being alone can be a positive one, depending on your outlook on life.

Being alone gives me time to decompress. I need time to sit and just stare out the window, or walk in the woods to clear my head from the day's activities. Don't get me wrong, I am a sociable kid, but I need time away from all the pettiness of being a teen to get a handle on myself.

—Boy, 15, Indiana

**I need to have time to just be alone in order to think. This seems weird to my parents. They expect me to want to be doing things with friends, but having down time to me is the greatest pleasure in my day. I can sort out some of the many ideas floating around in my head. Without time to do this, I get very moody and mean.**

**—Girl, 16, Florida**

Most of the time, I prefer to work alone on projects. This does cause some anxiety and concern in my classes when we have group activities. It's not that I don't like my peers. It just takes me time to mull over ideas before I can decide what to do. In group activities, people tend to pick the first thought that comes to mind to get the project done. I don't work that way. I want the best idea to be my choice for a project. This means I have to have time to decide amongst many thoughts. It is during my thinking time, in the quiet of my room, that my best and most interesting ideas emerge.

—Girl, 17, Scotland

**I aspire to be a novelist. This requires long periods of time developing characters and a solid plot line. This can only happen when I have the time to be alone and think. As a teen, it is difficult to protect my alone time. But, it is definitely a required part of my daily [routine].**

**—Boy, 17, Maine**

# INTERESTING OUTLIERS

This section reminds us of a beloved skit from one of our favorite British comedy shows, *Monty Python's Flying Circus*, "And, now for something completely different!"

Here are some individual comments from gifted teens that leave us in awe. They might not be representative of a large portion of the gifted population who responded to our online questionnaires, but these individual's concerns were poignant enough to warrant our attention.

(And, for the moment, don't worry, it is *not* time for the penguin on top of your television to explode!)

You should have asked how other people's beliefs about abilities could cause harm to gifted kids. I was diagnosed with ADHD at the age of 10 and put on medication. It let me stay focused on the boring stuff at school, but my creative ability just tanked. I used to have a wonderful imagination that helped me come up with interesting stories to write about. Now, I can barely stay mentally focused enough to slog through an assignment. My life is now about getting things done to get a grade. I don't have much pride in any of my work. It's just getting done.

—Boy, 13, Iowa

**Sibling rivalry is something you should have asked about. How do gifted kids get along with their brothers and sisters? What conflicts occur due to their giftedness? Do parents favor one child over another due to giftedness?**

**—Girl, 13, Florida**

You should have asked about competitiveness. Does being gifted mean you always have to outdo other people to show you are smart? Are there ways to show giftedness without having to win competitions?

—Boy, 14, Mississippi

**You should ask about *pressure*. How many gifties are out there who are pushed and prodded to get involved in everything? Clubs, sports, community organizations, church. In some ways, I feel like I am supposed to save the world because I'm gifted. I'm just a kid, I tell myself, but this doesn't seem good enough for other people. Why are gifted kids supposed to save the world? We didn't mess it up in the first place!**

**—Girl, 14, Kentucky**

You could ask about how teens might hide their abilities to go along with the crowd or be accepted. How do teens decide when to be themselves or find a way to not care about whether they fit in or not?

—Girl, 15, Virginia

Getting involved in online worlds allows me to escape the drudgery of my life as a high school student. I can take risks I would never think of doing in the real world, and I can experience things way beyond what my family thinks is appropriate for my age. How do other gifted kids experience life through social media or online gaming? Do they think this is going to change how we live our lives in the future? How has their experience changed their lives already? These are important questions I want to know more about.
—Boy, 15, Indiana

Ask what ways gifted kids get advanced experiences in an area they are interested in. Who supports them in meeting a mentor? How to go about getting an internship or job shadow? These are things I want to know more about. Especially how other gifted kids have experienced these things.
—Boy, 16, Pennsylvania

# YOUR TURN

From pressure to work to one's potential (whatever *that* means!) to fitting in with peers, stress is a common factor associated with being human—let alone gifted. Yet this state of mind seems to have special significance for gifted teens. It comes up in every conversation we have with gifted teens.

Split a piece of paper into two columns. One represents Negative Stress—that state of emotional distress that causes bad feelings. The other column on the paper represents Positive Stress—that state of emotional excitement that propels you forward.

Start listing examples of both negative and positive stress in your life in the appropriate columns. Which column is easier to fill in? Why?

Is destressing yourself important? How can you (or others) gain a more positive outlook on stress in your (their) life?

You should ask about how gifted people are making their local communities better places to live. You should ask about how adults have supported and helped get an idea off the ground and into motion. You should ask about how gifted kids keep a positive outlook on life.

—Girl, 16, Alabama

I'm not sure what the question is, but the answer is "humor." Humor is incredibly important; it's how you get through each day. Some things are so biased that if you can't find some way to laugh yourself through them, they will drag you down forever.

—Boy, 17, Virginia

# THE EIGHT GREAT GRIPES OF GIFTED KIDS

We end this chapter with a focus on some common concerns about giftedness that literally hundreds of gifted children and teens have commented about. The goal is to bring some humor (as the aforementioned 17-year-old Virginian points out) to the concerns teens continue to have about giftedness.

We also, though, take seriously the lack of clear answers that keep the questions and comments coming. Indeed, we wonder why it seems to be so difficult for the gifted to get answers to the questions they have from adults in their lives.

More than 20 years ago, authors Judy Galbraith and Jim Delisle (1996) concocted "The Eight Great Gripes," a listing of items that gifted kids and teens said they experienced frequently in their lives. Over those two decades, each of these gripes has withstood the test of time, as each one still applies to some segment of the gifted population.

# YOUR TURN

Read over the list below, circling any of the gripes that apply in your life, while crossing out any of the items that you don't believe apply to you. Next, for each item that you circled, write a brief explanation/elaboration as to your reasons for circling this gripe.

1. No one explains what being "smart" or "gifted" is all about. It's kept a big mystery.
2. School is too easy and not challenging.
3. Parents, teachers, and/or friends expect me to be perfect at everything.
4. Friends who really understand me are hard to find.
5. Kids often tease me about being smart.
6. I feel overwhelmed by the number of things I can do in life.
7. I feel different and alienated from most of my class-mates—I think in different ways than they do.
8. I worry about world problems and feel helpless to do anything about them.

We've listed some examples below of how a selection of gifted teens recently responded to each of the gripes. How do these responses match up with your experiences?

## GRIPE #1
**No one explains what being "smart" or "gifted" is all about. It's kept a big mystery.**

★ Anyone who is not in gifted classes thinks gifted is syn-onymous with "smart people," which means that if they don't consider themselves "smart," they look down on anyone who is. Often, I have been prejudged as being arrogant by a person who doesn't even know me, just because of my "gifted" label. That's why I don't talk about being in gifted classes.

- ★ You tell us that we are "gifted," but you never define the term. What's *that* all about?

- ★ In fourth grade, I took a test to determine if I was gifted. Seven years later, I still don't know the qualifications.

- ★ When I was tested for giftedness when I was younger, I was told it meant that I was "special." What's *that* supposed to mean?

- ★ When I came home from my first day of kindergarten, my mom asked if I had made any friends. I told her I thought I would be friends with the teacher, because we were the only ones who could read. Since then, it's been pretty much like that . . .

## GRIPE #2

**School is too easy and not challenging.**

- ★ School is difficult because of the *quantity* of work, not its *quality*. The material itself is simple, standard, and almost always lacks application.

- ★ School is just like seeing your life pass by without even watching it. I constantly zone out to something more interesting.

- ★ School is "one size fits all." It caters more to kids who are slower, not gifted kids. I get bored in school almost every day.

## GRIPE #3

**Parents, teachers, and/or friends expect me to be perfect at everything.**

- ★ One of my teachers actually said I'm a beacon of hope in my class. I feel like if I don't do well on something, I'm letting him down.

★ I'm human. Don't expect perfection from me unless you can dish it out yourself.

★ My friends expect me to be perfect, but my teachers and parents are more realistic.

★ Before I get a test back, I hear a lot of "Oh . . . I bet you got a perfect grade." No! I don't get "perfects." It's irritating.

## GRIPE #4
**Friends who really understand me are hard to find.**

★ When I'm in a class with none of my gifted friends, I have trouble with things like working in groups. I have nothing in common with other students, and we don't have the same styles of learning.

★ My "nongifted" friends find it hard to relate to me on an intellectual level. But, I can truly be myself around other gifted kids.

★ . . . boring small talk. It's just the same old things all the time. I need friends who can talk to me on a deeper level and not be intimidated by my skills.

★ People who are "average" don't understand me, but gifted kids are so unique that they aren't like me either. Hmmm . . .

★ Kids in high school are really superficial. Which is why I tend to stay away from nongifted people.

## GRIPE #5
**Kids often tease me about being smart.**

★ Kids often ask why I didn't get 100% on something. I feel like they should be more concerned about why *they* didn't get 100%, considering my GPA is probably higher than theirs.

★ Teasing is more intense when I fail.

★ Because I have trouble working in groups, I often work by myself if that's a choice. But then, people think I am making fun of them or that I am better than they are. It's maddening.

## GRIPE #6
**I feel overwhelmed by the number of things I can do in life.**

★ I have no idea what I want to do when I get older—there are so many places I want to go, personally. It *is* overwhelming!

★ I wouldn't say I'm *overwhelmed* by my choices, but more just constantly redivided. One month, I was adamant that my future job would be in Japan. Now, I'm looking at Germany and other EU nations. All these possibilities are amazing, but which one I want, which one will make me happy, is a question I may not answer until I get out of school.

★ I am proud to be in gifted classes and to have all the opportunities that come with them, but it's hard to know which talents to perfect and which ones to leave as hobbies. Still, I *like* having many talents and hobbies.

★ I've considered so many jobs it isn't even funny. I made a list of things that I *don't* want to be because it is shorter than that of my interests.

★ I don't know where I want to go. Vaguely, med school, but I'd be just as happy in any job where I can help and inspire people.

## GRIPE #7

**I feel different and alienated from most of my classmates—I think in different ways than they do.**

★ I'm not like most kids. I don't like sports, TV, or pop music. Because of this and my abstract mind, I often feel that I am totally alone.

★ I feel bad when I think differently and understand stuff no one around me understands.

★ Having to dumb my thoughts down infuriates me. The deeper meanings are lost when I do this.

★ Nobody has the exact same thoughts, but there are plenty of people with the "cheerleader" mindset or the "jock" mindset. I guess you could say there aren't many with a "gifted" mindset . . .

## GRIPE #8

**I worry about world problems and feel helpless to do anything about them.**

★ I think everyone has one thing they feel strongly about. More than anything else for me, that is the environment and humans' impact on it. I feel like everyone else is blind. I can see everything that is going wrong with the Earth, but everyone else just looks away and pretends to worry about the economy and "more important" issues. Those people are the ones who will kill this planet simply because they are too afraid of facing the facts. They refuse to accept that if they want to let the Earth recover, they might not be able to drive their gas-guzzling SUVs.

★ I want a better place, like a fantasy world from a book or video game, but I know our world will never be like that. It will either become better with time, or it will just become more used to its demise. No matter how I see it, the world may need fixing, but I don't know just how to fix it.

★ Seeing a problem that you may have a solution to, or an idea for a solution, is hard, but nobody really wants to listen to a 13–16-year-old's plans to fix something.

★ The government wouldn't be so bad if there were children as representatives or consultants. We see things differently, which might be helpful.

★ I constantly worry about world issues, and I think of every outcome possible and how it would affect my life and my family.

★ One person, too many problems, not enough time. Some people don't even bother to listen to kids like us.

# YOUR TURN

Really. *Your turn.*

We have provided ample opportunity for you to learn about yourself through our subtle nudging in the Your Turn activities throughout this book. Yet, we know there are always important questions and concerns that seem to go unanswered or unaddressed in the attempt to deal broadly with issues and ideas.

What questions or concerns about being gifted and growing up should have been asked and answered in this book? What is on *your* mind now that you've heard what others have to say?

We want to know what you want to know about. Add your voice to the conversation. Visit our website (http://www.giftedkidspeak.com) and take part in the ongoing questionnaire discussion. Or, if you prefer a more personal approach, you can reach us at: learninglatitudes@giftedkidspeak.com.

—Bob Schultz and Jim Delisle

# REFERENCES

Broome, C. (2011, October). The power of teachers: Imogene Hill turned Jobs' won't into will. Retrieved from http://guess what.rugbyjones.com/2011/10/the-power-of-teachers-imogene-hill-turned-jobs-wont-into-will

cummings, e.e. (1955). A poet's advice to students. *Journal of Humanistic Psychology, 12*(2), 75.

*Erma Bombeck.* (n.d.). Retrieved from http://www.goodreads.com/quotes/show/209784

Galbraith, J., & Delisle, J. (1996). *The gifted kids' survival guide: A teen handbook.* Minneapolis, MN: Free Spirit.

Johnson, B. (2011, October 1). *September 26–October 2: L. A. Reid explains why he dropped Lady Gaga from Island Def Jam.* Retrieved from http://music.yahoo.com/blogs.thats-really-week/134460/september-26-october-2-la-reid-explains-why-he-dropped-lady-gaga-from-island-def-jam.html

Kaufmann, F. A. (1980). A follow-up study of the 1964–1968 presidential scholars. (Doctoral dissertation). *Dissertation Abstracts International, 40A,* 5794A.

Laudau, E. (2010, August 6). *Lady Gaga went to geek camp, too.* Retrieved from http://articles.cnn.com/2010-08-06/living/geek.camp.talented_1_programs-for-gifted-students-three-week-session-talented-youth?_s=PM:LIVING

*Mayim Bialik's brainiac advantage.* (2011, October 2). Retrieved from http://www.parade.com/celebrity/personality-parade/2011/10/mayim-bialik.html

Tietz, J. (2011, December 8). Santiago's brain. *Rolling Stone,* 78–87.

# ABOUT THE AUTHORS

**Robert A. Schultz, Ph.D.**, is professor of gifted education and curriculum studies at the University of Toledo in Ohio, where he directs the CIGI (Curriculum and Instruction Gifted) program and coordinates doctoral programs in curriculum and instruction and early childhood education. A man of many hats, Bob also travels the country as a consultant in gifted education and curriculum development/evaluation, working with families and teachers addressing social/emotional needs of the gifted and developing education plans for gifted and highly/profoundly gifted individuals; teaches in public schools; and conducts research in and writes about giftedness—especially from the perspective of children, teens, and young adults (he has more than 100 articles and book chapters and two books under his belt). Most importantly, he is better known as Dad to his kids.

Bob and his wife, Cindy, live in Waterville, OH, but hope to one day while away their time sailing in the Caribbean supported by their children (*did you hear that, kids?*). Until then, Bob plans to continue helping parents, teachers, and school districts meet the diverse needs of gifted learners in and out of classrooms.

**James R. Delisle, Ph.D.**, has worked with gifted teens for more than 30 years as a teacher and counselor. Jim is also an avid writer, having published 17 books, seven of which were written specifically for gifted kids and teens (the rest are for teachers and parents). His best-selling book *The Gifted Teen Survival Guide* (coauthored with Judy Galbraith) was even highlighted on the Oprah show. Jim received his Ph.D. when he was 28 years old and went on to become a college professor for the next 27 years. While teaching at the university level, Jim took time one day each week to teach in a gifted program in an Ohio public school.

In his retirement, Jim splits his time between North Myrtle Beach, SC, and Washington, DC. Jim's wife, Deb, serves as the nation's Assistant Secretary of Elementary and Secondary Education at the United States Department of Education. Their son, Matt, is a special effects editor who cuts and splices Hollywood movies, MTV videos, and TV ads for major companies and professional sports teams. Jim plans to walk as many beaches as he can find and to write whenever the mood strikes him to do so.